Innovative Games

Brenda Lichtman, PhD

Sam Houston State University
Huntsville, Texas

Human Kinetics Publishers

Library of Congress Cataloging-in-Publication Data

Lichtman, Brenda, 1948-
      Innovative games / Brenda Lichtman.
          p.   cm.
      Includes index.
      ISBN 0-87322-488-4
      1. Physical education for children. 2. Games.   I. Title.
      GV443.L5   1993
      372.86--dc20   93-20454
                                                                                                    CIP

ISBN: 0-87322-488-4

Copyright © 1993 by Brenda Lichtman

The following activities were introduced to the author or adapted from activities at Camps Kenwood–Evergreen, Potter Place, NH: Bucket Brigade, Continuous Capture the Flag, Human Anagrams, and Treasure Hunt.

Acquisitions Editor: Rick Frey, PhD; Developmental Editor: Mary E. Fowler; Assistant Editors: Dawn Roselund, Lisa Sotirelis, and John Wentworth; Copyeditor: Ginger Rodriguez; Proofreaders: Karin Leszczynski and Julia Anderson; Indexer: Theresa J. Schaefer; Production Director: Ernie Noa; Typesetter: Angela K. Snyder; Text Design: Jody Boles; Text Layout: Tara Welsch; Cover Design: Jack Davis; Interior Art: Tim Offenstein and Gretchen Walters; Printer: Versa Press

Human Kinetics books are available at special discounts for bulk purchase. Special editions or book excerpts can also be created to specification. For details, contact the Special Sales Manager at Human Kinetics.

Printed in the United States of America   10   9   8   7   6   5   4   3   2

Human Kinetics
P.O. Box 5076, Champaign, IL 61825-5076
1-800-747-4457

Canada: Human Kinetics, Box 24040, Windsor, ON N8Y 4Y9
1-800-465-7301 (in Canada only)

Europe: Human Kinetics, P.O. Box IW14, Leeds LS16 6TR, England
(44) 532 781708

Australia: Human Kinetics, 2 Ingrid Street, Clapham 5062, South Australia
(08) 371 3755·

New Zealand: Human Kinetics, P.O. Box 105-231, Auckland 1
(09) 309 2259

that the creative person has an ability to think in a divergent manner and a skill for integrating information in a unique way that produces a fresh approach. For many experts, innovation is the key ingredient in creativity.

Most people believe that creativity is desirable, yet as Ralph Waldo Emerson pointed out in "The American Scholar" in 1837 (Porte, 1983, pp. 58-59), schools and colleges in the 19th century often did little to foster its development, drilling students rather than requiring them to synthesize and integrate facts.

Even after 150 years of supposed progress within our schools, Silberman (1970), Holt (1974), Sarason (1990), Schlechty (1990), and Toch (1991) claimed not much has changed. Schools barely tolerate divergent behavior and thinking through the early elementary grades, and they offer little positive reinforcement for its continuation. Rather, children are taught in both subtle and direct ways that conformity is more desirable. When the child who uses a blue crayon to draw a tree trunk is reminded that trees are brown, or when the person who questions why the let rules in badminton and tennis are different is told, "That's just the way those sports are played," we are sending the message that we reward more highly thinking that meshes with the norm. In the process, we are destroying our children's curiosity and desire to think or act independently.

This problem extends beyond everyday program decision making to the make-up of the entire curriculum. We are reluctant to allow students greater responsibility in making decisions about content. Yet, as Bok (1986) points out in *Higher Learning*,

> More and more, the United States will have to live by its wits, prospering or declining according to the capacity of its people to develop new ideas, to work with sophisticated technology, to create new products and imaginative new ways of solving problems. Of all our national assets, a trained intelligence and a capacity for innovation and discovery seem destined to be the most important. (jacket cover)

The world is beseiged with enormously difficult issues that will need to be confronted in novel ways because standard solutions no longer work: crime, drug abuse, ecological concerns, a limited health-care system, and economic problems.

Tye and Novotney (1975) were sensitive to this issue when they wrote that

> for the educator, the problem is clear: how can the children of today be educated to live in the world that hardly can be imagined but which will be upon us with appalling rapidity? Clearly, our traditional approach to schooling will not be adequate to handle the task,

Encouraging Creativity | 1

When was the last time your students came to you brimming with enthusiasm, asking, "What activities are we going to play today?" If you're like most physical education and recreation instructors, you can't remember such an instance.

We could make a difference in disinterested attitudes by expanding our usual yearly program evaluations and looking at our curricular offerings from the participants' point of view. We may see our curricula as varied when in fact they present the same activities year after year. In large part the content of our learning units is very similar across grades 6 to 12—rewarming skills, revisiting standard strategies, and rehashing rules. And the problem is fueled because many of the same activities are offered in community-based recreation leagues, intramurals, and interscholastic sports. Viewed in this light, is it surprising that many teenagers perceive organized activity programs as the same old stuff?

Our activity programs must compete with the dozens of entertainment choices young people have at their fingertips. If choice and variety are part of the key to keeping adolescents' interest high, our curricular offerings must diversify to avoid what I call the "oh, that again" syndrome, which produces a seeming lack of motivation in participants. The cure lies in the periodic infusion of novel activities. Although such additions are not a panacea, they can help break the standard repetitive cycle, while providing variety and a sense of freshness to program offerings.

Does this mean that we should abandon the traditional activities— basketball, volleyball, softball, and the like? Absolutely not, for these sports provide valuable skills and knowledge and help to shape desirable affective behaviors. But if we hope to instill in our participants a love of movement that they will carry throughout their lives, we need to spice up our programs, making them more innovative and less predictable. And at the same time, we can meet our overall goals and objectives.

Unlocking Creativity, Discovering Innovation

Many theorists have struggled to devise a clear and concise definition of creativity (Adams, 1986; Haefele, 1962; Mooney & Razik, 1967; Ochse, 1990; Parnes & Harding, 1962; Shank, 1988; Steinberg, 1988). They imply

Acknowledgments

Writing any textbook requires the efforts of many people who have worked behind the scenes. The innovative games classes that I have taught to undergraduate and graduate students have been an inspiration, and they continue to plant the seeds for new games ideas. In serving as guinea pigs for my creations, my students have been a patient audience and astute critics. Their suggstions have assisted me in modifying games and making them more effective.

Linda Barajas, Janet McCullough, Donna Smith, and Karen Wright aided in the arduous task of transcribing my handwritten words into handouts for my classes that provided the foundation for this book. Their patience in typing rewrite after rewrite was commendable.

The "Game" description provides you with the most pertinent details for successfully introducing the activity. Any exceptions to rules that carry over from well-known activities are noted, and any stipulations regarding concern for safety are reinforced. For most team activities, you can easily draw from your own experiences and apply them, but if an innovative activity does not have a traditional model, its specifics are explained in detail.

Competitive activities can result in injury, regardless of the degree to which you exercise prudent restraint. Unique "Safety Considerations" are addressed, but, as a professional, you must ensure that general safety precautions are followed.

The requirements for the activities in *Innovative Games* are not etched in stone. Unlike traditional games, these don't have years of exposure that have honed them to a precise form. Use the activities in whatever ways are best for you and those you instruct, making the modifications needed for your situation.

To assist you with creating new games, I have identified six principles on which innovative games can be developed. By understanding and applying one or a combination of these principles, you and your students will be able to devise your own innovative activities. In doing so, you can foster your participants' interests and reinforce the processes underlying divergent thinking and the devising of novel ideas. Perhaps you'll never again hear a student say "oh, that again."

Preface

Physical educators and recreation professionals face an enormous challenge: how to achieve our objectives yet keep motivation high enough to avoid the "oh, that again" syndrome (an infectious malady common in programs that rely too heavily on the triad of volleyball, basketball, and softball). Many curricula rehash activities that students have experienced year after year. It is no wonder that boredom results.

One cure for curriculum and program stagnation is an infusion of innovative activities into the more standard or traditional sport units. Meeting psychomotor objectives also is important. To reach the dual objective of achieving psychomotor goals while keeping motivation high, you need to know the principles from which you can develop creative games and activities. With these concepts in mind, you—and even your students—can devise your own innovative activities.

In *Innovative Games* you will find 35 games that can be integrated immediately into programs for children in grades 6 through 12. Any equipment not already available can be solicited from local merchants, purchased at garage sales, or collected from participants' families. Equipment needs are listed for the number of active participants in each game.

The activities are organized in a consistent, easy-to-follow format. After a brief overview, the "Objectives" section identifies the goals that each activity seeks to develop, ensures accountability, and helps curriculum planners understand where best to integrate the game into the existing program.

"Helpful Hints" offers game variations along with alterations to make games less difficult or more challenging, depending on the needs of the participants. For those who provide activities for upper elementary school children, an "Adaptations for Younger Participants" section is included for many of the games. A "Variations" section is included when an idea from one innovative activity can be applied in a different setting, but requires explanation of how the rules and regulations must be altered.

"Playing Area" indicates the type of facility best suited for the activity. A number of the games employ spaces typically underused by most schools and recreational facilities. In about a quarter of the games, large numbers of participants can be accommodated in a relatively small area. "Participants" specifies the number of active players and, where applicable, identifies their positions or roles. Also listed is the number of officials needed for the activity to progress smoothly.

Contents

To my parents, who encouraged me to explore, provided me with opportunities to experience, and allowed me the freedom to create.

and we must begin now to restructure our educational system. The question is, what implications do these projections of the future hold for schools and in which directions should today's educators begin their planning? (p. 19)

As professionals, we must change our focus to emphasize innovative approaches that provide plausible solutions and offer unique possibilities.

Creativity: An Elusive Term

We use the term *creativity* without a second thought, but a precise description is difficult to pin down. Reber's (1985) approach seems most workable. She considers creativity "a mental process that leads to solutions, ideas, conceptualizations, artistic forms, theories or products that are unique and novel" (p. 28). This process involves the ability to generalize relationships, to bridge conceptual gaps, and ultimately leads to creation, which in turn results in something useful that did not exist before. The inventor devises new products after careful choices, rather than by some rote or iterative process.

Creativity depends upon motive and opportunity. Research suggests that besides taking risks and having spontaneity, independence, self-confidence, liveliness, impulsiveness, and high tolerance of ambiguity, creative individuals are intrinsically motivated. They gain satisfaction from engaging in the creative process, which serves as an end in itself. Although they take pleasure in the result, the product or tangible reward is not their driving force (Haefele, 1962; Shank, 1988; Steinberg, 1988). If you encourage adolescents to devise novel games, you help them look at problems in alternative ways, a major component of creativity, while also getting the chance to enjoy the fruits of their labor.

The Professional's Role

Do you encourage a "coloring book" approach to thinking? Preset outlines strangle creativity by requiring a person to stay within the fixed lines. We need to provide an atmosphere in which individuals are willing to attempt to develop new games. At the same time, we must keep in mind that the games don't have to be perfect to possess intrinsic value. Those who we lead and teach are not on a mission to invent the next sport to be adopted by the Olympics. Your goal is to have participants devise activities that differ from the standard fare to which they have been exposed. By following the simple guidelines in Figure 1.1, we can help adolescents achieve this objective.

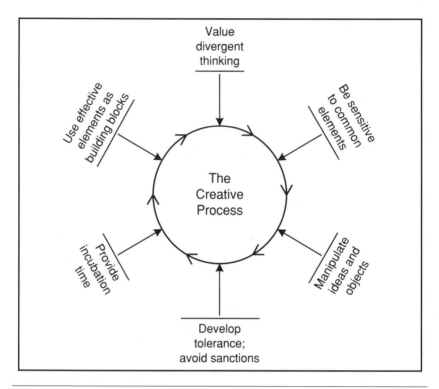

Figure 1.1   Guidelines for encouraging creativity.

Value Divergent Thinking

Unless you place a premium on developing innovative games, participants are not likely to spend the time and effort required for this creative endeavor. By encouraging exploration of different approaches to accomplishing a specific objective, you provide an open environment where experimentation is valued. Setting an example by devising your own new activities, or at least selecting and implementing games students have not played before, is essential. By doing this you'll reinforce their desire and pique their curiosity to experience different activities.

Be Sensitive to Common Elements

Make participants more sensitive to their environment and the common elements that comprise a game to promote creativity. Obviously, every game must possess a goal or objective, but if you define it precisely from the start, you stifle, rather than enhance, the creative process. Imagine trying to think in global terms if the stated goal was that "players try to score points by kicking a soccer ball through the uprights of a football goal post." You would focus on soccer. By substituting the objective of propelling a ball into an area defined as a target or goal, you open up limitless possibilities. Once the goal is identified, a series of questions like those in Table 1.1 can be posed that will serve to determine the major elements of the activity.

Manipulate Ideas and Objects

Identifying the activity's strengths and shortcomings is the next step. Your group's analysis should be balanced; if you pay attention to only the negative aspects and ignore positive features, you risk curing a problem while detracting from a desirable feature. You should devise and test more than one solution for a problem and choose the most effective one. After you eliminate the major pitfalls, address some of the less critical factors. Finally, fine-tune the game by playing it.

Table 1.1 Factors to Consider During the Games Creation Process

Major element	Questions
Goal	What is the general objective? What method(s) exist for scoring?
Equipment	What items? How many? Any special requirements? Other materials and supplies?
Playing area	What facilities? Are these critical? Does selection impact the equipment to be used? Facility size and layout? Special markings and their functions? Where are goals to be positioned?
Participants	Is there a minimum, maximum, or ideal number? What are the player positions and their responsibilities? Do players assume a specific configuration? Are other people needed, such as scorers or referees?
Game	What method(s) of locomotion? Are there any special requirements? What rules are needed? What is required in the general flow of the activity? How is success or winning determined?
Safety concerns	Are there any special safety considerations? Can the game be made safer by altering the rules, changing the equipment, changing court set-up, and so on? If changes are made, how will they impact the game?

Develop Tolerance and Avoid Sanctions

Novel activities often require unique rules, player set-ups, court design, and so on. It may be inappropriate to use preexisting patterns from traditional sports or even other innovative games. Yet at the same time, you don't need to reinvent the whole wheel each time you create a new activity. If you reward students for adopting a what-if attitude and reinforce it with your let's-try-it approach, you will send a clear message that using elements that seem to have worked in similar situations is fine, but allowing imaginations to devise unique, but workable, solutions is also valued.

Often people misinterpret constructive criticism, believing that criticism is directed at them personally rather than at an idea. To encourage an open dialogue, you must make it clear that eliminating a particular aspect of an activity does not mean that the person who suggested it is stupid, for the same idea might be perfect in a different activity setting. It is extremely important to realize that there is no absolute formula to apply to the process of creation or to modification of original ideas. Rather, it takes a good dose of educated guesswork to smooth out the glitches.

Provide Incubation Time

Time is a critical factor in the creative process; ideas need to simmer to some degree before they can be translated into a workable form. Small-group discussion is an ideal way to plant the seeds that grow to novel ideas, but without time for personal introspection and consideration, end products may not be as rich or as well thought-out as possible. Reluctance to sacrifice activity time for group interchange is understandable, but sharing is essential for the developmental process to proceed. Perhaps you could devote part of a rainy day or study hall to this task. When a lesson or practice calls for station work, consider including a "think tank" station where the elements of a novel activity can be devised or fine-tuned. In school settings, homework could be assigned or informal interchange could be encouraged in locker rooms, in transit to playing fields, and during lunch periods.

Use Effective Elements as Building Blocks

Football and baseball undergo rule changes almost annually. Naismith's version of basketball was a far cry from the game we know today. In other words, games undergo continual evolution. But new developments aren't necessarily good ones. What do you do if, after careful consideration and even a consensus among group members, some suggestions or even entire games just don't seem to work?

First, don't automatically throw the baby out with the bath water. Elements can surely be salvaged and used as the nucleus to devise an alternative that does function successfully. Second, what you might be tempted to judge a dismal failure need not be viewed in such absolute terms. There is inherent value in engaging adolescents in the constructive process of thinking and devising unique alternatives to standard curriculum offerings that will impact their physical education and recreational experiences. By doing so you change the psychological emphasis in the gymnasium setting from passive to active cognitive processing. Success in creating a new game is not defined merely in terms of the utilitarian function of the product, but in the effort and motivation expended to push back the barriers that all too often confine our thinking. It is this pushing back and opening up that helps us define ourselves by making us aware of what we are capable of accomplishing and allows individuals the freedom to explore and expand their thinking.

Where Do You Start?

There may be psychological safety in continuing with "the same old stuff," but the SOS approach spells danger. It erects a barrier against change, and the fear of failure prevents us from becoming risk-takers. Nothing awful will come if you are wrong or if things don't go as smoothly as planned. Isn't it better to try and fail than to do nothing? Help provide participants the motivation they need to begin by introducing games they haven't experienced, offering them the opportunity to engage in the creative process, and encouraging and recognizing their efforts.

Broaden Experiences

Your first step will be to broaden the activities in your curriculum or program. This should enhance learners' interest and provide meaning and value. Start by introducing a few of the games described in chapters 2 through 7. These include

- developing hybrid activities by melding elements from two or more standard sports or games,
- using nontraditional equipment such as trash cans, plastic half-gallon jugs, and the like as an integral part of a game,
- altering locomotion and manipulation,
- modifying the goal of a typical activity or using a unique player set-up,
- finding new uses for standard equipment, and
- creating activities by adapting ideas from multimedia presentations (television, films, videos, arcade and board games, etc.).

This last principle provides an excellent place to begin. The typical American watches television for close to 4 hours per day (Dietz & Gortmaker, 1985), and game shows such as "Wheel of Fortune," "Jeopardy," and "American Gladiators" are especially popular. You can capitalize on some of the interest in these games by incorporating elements from them in your program. Basic requirements of some of the challenges posed on "American Gladiators," for example, can be lifted and modified to gentler and more appropriate forms. The event in which a contestant is required to swing on a set of rings to a goal area without being knocked off the rings is simply a form of tag using a novel means of locomotion. Couldn't you create an alternative using innovative locomotor patterns that aren't as hazardous? Another "American Gladiators" challenge requires the contestant to hit a target before being hit. Doesn't that seem very much like high tech bombardment? What if players aimed at inanimate objects? You can modify the goal to make it approrpiate while keeping the excitement of the game.

Create a Games Book

One useful project is to devise a games book of the activities participants develop. Future groups can play the games, which will also serve as models for creations by other classes. Having models is critical, for initially teenagers will reflect society's pervasive attitudes: "If it's not broken don't attempt to fix it" and "It probably won't work or someone would have thought of it before." These ideas filter down from the highest administrative levels to our clientele. The games book can convince others that devising novel activities is not reserved only for those who possess special gifts. When adolescents realize that their peers played an integral role in developing a novel activity you introduced to them, they seem to shed their negative mindset for a more positive and self-assured attitude.

Direct Small-Group Brainstorming

Once a few shows or videos have been identified as the building blocks upon which innovative games can be developed, divide into small groups of four to five people each. You can assign a program or video game or let each group choose one to use as the springboard for its own game. If restrictions must be applied (for example, if the game has to be played in a given facility or a minimum number of participants must be accommodated), establish them at the very beginning. Let the brainstorming proceed for 5 to 10 minutes. The goal at this point is to identify the basic elements of the new activity, not to refine them. Provide incubation time by assigning participants to think about the ideas that were discussed within the group. At the next opportunity, have group members exchange their thoughts and settle on one avenue to pursue in greater detail.

Once the major elements have been identified, the group should present the outline of the activity to the instructor. You should scrutinize the game for any obvious safety hazards and offer feedback about them, but avoid suggesting solutions. Instead, ask the group to arrive at viable alternatives. Do not point out other weaknesses. While it is tempting and perhaps expedient to do so, it will defeat part of your purpose. Once the safety issues are resolved, allow the group no more than 5 to 10 minutes to try out its creation. Glaring shortcomings will become obvious.

At the third meeting, let the group modify the activity to rectify the problems or at least reduce them to a tolerable level. Provide additional opportunities for small-group participation to determine if the suggestions were successful in ameliorating the major problems.

Once the group has reached this point, usually at a fourth meeting, it is time to describe and demonstrate the activity to the other groups. Unless the group includes an older high school student, you will probably want to explain the activity yourself rather than give that responsibility to a group member. Again, 5 to 10 minutes of play are adequate and will allow participants to ask questions and provide additional feedback. This feedback is the foundation for further modifications. The process of implementing suggestions and analyzing their consequences will, in most cases, alter the activity to produce a viable program option.

The Additive Approach to Game Creation

Another technique to use in a small-group setting is an additive method for developing a novel activity. In this approach, each person in a group defines one element in the innovative activity. These elements might include playing area, equipment, object of the game, number of players, players' general responsibilities and positioning, and the type of locomotor patterns permitted.

So in the additive approach, the first person might decide that the game is to take place on a soccer field, and the second elects to use baseball bats, whiffle balls, and trash cans. The third individual decides how this equipment could be used in that setting; one alternative would be to hit whiffle balls fungo-style into the trash cans. The next person would determine the flow of this activity by deciding whether it would be a cooperative effort or a competitive game for two teams. In the case of competition, members of both teams could hit balls over the midfield line to their team's designated trash can targets. Shaggers could return balls that did not score a goal. Cooperation would be the major focus if the same configuration were used but the entire group worked together over a set period of time to improve upon the previous best score.

Once the basic plan for the activity is devised, participants will need to experiment with the actions to determine reasonable distances, how much equipment will be required, and what rules must be implemented so the game can progress smoothly and effectively. While refinement of the game is taking place, you should stress safety factors.

In the game just described, the activity changes the usual goal of batting, which typically does not require participants to project an object into a receptacle. Occasionally, use of this progressive developmental approach will result in an activity that integrates two or more principles rather than using only one. You will need to monitor the actions carefully, pointing out potential difficulties if players are not sensitive to them and offering suggestions and feedback where needed.

Before the Games Begin

We often are reluctant to try things that are different from the ordinary. We accept the "if it's not broken, don't fix it" attitude. Unfortunately, the price for our reluctance is often an outbreak of the "oh that again," syndrome.

My intent in outlining the philosophy, principles, and games in this book is not to upset the apple cart. Rather, it is my hope that while keeping the tried and true stock, but adding variety on occasion, we can keep our physical education and recreation classes vibrant and fresh. Let the games begin.

Developing Hybrid Activities | 2

When you merge elements from two or more standard activities, the end product is a different game from its foundations. This approach for devising innovative curricular offerings is not only easy to understand, but the possibilities are almost limitless.

The simplest way to visualize potential pairings is to draw a matrix similar to the one in Table 2.1 The horizontal and vertical axes represent well-known sports.

Table 2.1   Schema for Developing Hybrid Activities

Well-known sport	Softball	Basketball	Volleyball	Soccer
Softball	—	Soft-basket	Soft-volley	Soft-goalball*
Basketball	—	—	Basket-volley	Spasketball*
Volleyball	—	—	—	Volley-soccer*
Soccer	—	—	—	—

*These hybrids appear within this chapter.

Although the combinations identified in Table 2.1 either have been developed or appear to be promising, obviously not all combinations are feasible. For example, if you merged volleyball and field hockey and required players to use a field hockey stick to propel a volleyball over a net, the game may not be successful. Chapter 6, which discusses modified uses of standard equipment, suggests playing field hockey with a volleyball, but the result would not be considered a hybrid activity because major elements from volleyball haven't been infused into the game.

Table 2.1 is not meant to be exhaustive; rather, it is intended to provide a conceptual method for creating hybrid activities. Furthermore, Table 2.1 only includes pairs of sports. Very often, elements from a third activity can, or in some cases must, be integrated in order to refine the new creation. Spasketball, which is included on pages 17 to 20, illustrates this by allowing court players three options for scoring using basketball, soccer, and team handball methods.

The Games

The activities that follow are ordered along a continuum based on the ease with which you can introduce them to participants who possess some basic motor skills and knowledge about the sports from which the hybrid is formed. In large part, this listing also coincides with the level of skill participants need for each activity to progress effectively.

Soft Goalball

By infusing the defensive skills of softball with the strategy and skills of soccer, an exciting, fast-paced game emerges in which players score goals by throwing (1 point) or kicking (3 points) a mush-type softball into a scaled-down soccer net.

Objectives: Develop catching, fielding, and throwing skills and reinforce soccer dribbling, passing, and strategy. Enhance speed, agility, and cardiorespiratory endurance.

Equipment: One foam or mush-type softball or a small playground ball, 11 pinnies, and chalk. Four cones and four 15-ft pieces of clothesline used to reduce the size of a standard field hockey or soccer goal. A softball or baseball glove for each player, although the glove is optional except for the goalies.

Playing Area: A field hockey or soccer field. Position a goal crease similar to that used in team handball in front of the goal with the penalty shot line 1 ft beyond the apex of the crease on the midfield side, as seen in Figure 2.1. Form a 12- to 16-ft goal width by tying a piece of rope between a pylon and the crossbar on each side of the opening.

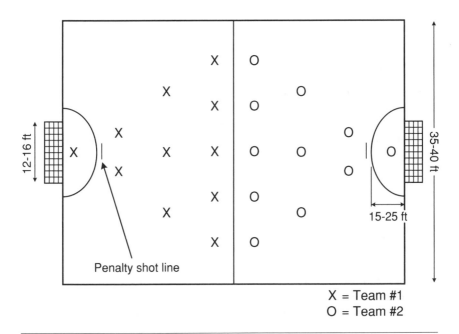

Figure 2.1   Soft Goalball field design and player set-up.

Participants: A minimum of 22 players, with the possible addition of another goalie per team depending on skill level. Two officials.

Game: The flow of the game and general rules are most similar to soccer, with the addition of being able to advance the ball down the field by throwing and air dribbling. To air dribble, a player repeatedly tosses the ball in the air and catches it while running or walking. As long as each toss is at a minimum of eye level and occurs at least once every three steps, the player can continue to advance the ball and not be guilty of traveling. Once a player has caught the ball from an air dribble and no longer uses the dribble-step-step-step pattern, he or she must throw or kick the ball to avoid a traveling violation.

Additional Rules: The following infractions result in an indirect free throw or kick. A member of the opposing team takes the ball at the spot where the violation occurred or on the goal crease line, whichever is closest. All players must be located at least 10 ft away, and the throw or kick must be completed within 5 sec.

- A player other than the goalie touches the ball in the goal crease.
- A player takes more than three steps holding the ball, without air dribbling at least once.
- A player stops and then resumes the toss-step-step-step locomotor pattern for air dribbling without having another player touch the ball.
- After a goalie throw or an indirect throw or kick from the goal crease line, a field player doesn't touch the ball before it crosses the centerline.
- A closely guarded player holds the ball for more than 5 sec. (The same rules as basketball apply.)
- A player uses more than two air dribbles before throwing the ball inbounds from the sidelines. Other than this rule, no other stipulations pertain to an out-of-bounds play.

Other Soft Goalball violations have different results.

- Should the ball become trapped by members of opposing teams, the two players complete a jump ball, as in basketball, at the spot of the tie-up with all other players located at least 10 ft away.
- Entry into the goal crease area by a member of the defensive team for defending purposes results in a corner throw unless the shot on goal is blocked and would, in the official's judgment, have resulted in a score. In that case, the offensive player takes a penalty shot. Repeated violations of the goal crease area by the defense can result in a penalty throw at the referee's discretion.

- Entry into the goal crease area by a member of the offensive team negates any shot on goal and results in the goalie putting the ball in play.

Safety Considerations: To reduce the possibility of two players colliding, players should avoid throwing the ball over long distances unless the receiver will be able to secure the ball without a defender interfering. Encourage players to field ground balls using their glove, if one is provided, particularly if an opponent is approaching who might attempt to kick the ball.

Helpful Hints: Person-to-person guarding is essential, and it follows the same marking pattern used in soccer. Encourage players to use ground balls to score goals as well as drop kicks. Ground balls are particularly effective when the offense passes the ball quickly from one side of the crease to the other.

If you use more than one goalie, they should work together and decide on appropriate coverage of the area. When one goalie stops a ball, the other goalie should run toward the top of the crease to get the ball from the goalie who made the save and hopefully catch the opposing team in a defensive lapse.

Volley-Tennis

Enhance volleyball action by allowing players to return the ball after a single bounce over a net lowered to tennis height. Consult "Adaptations for Younger Participants" for modifications for fourth and fifth graders.

Objectives: Develop all volleyball skills except overhand and sidearm serves. Emphasis placed on spiking because the net is at the 3-ft level.

Equipment: One volleyball and masking tape.

Playing Area: A tennis or volleyball court with the net lowered to 3 ft. When using a tennis court, tape a serving line 11 ft in back of the service line as shown in Figure 2.2.

Participants: From 6 to 12 people per team depending on the size of the playing area and the skill level of the players. One referee per court.

Game: Action proceeds as in traditional volleyball with the following exceptions. The ball can be played on the volley as in volleyball or after it has bounced once between two players' hits. Players must use only underhand serves. For younger and less skillful participants, move the serving line forward as deemed necessary. With highly skilled players, require that all spikes be taken with the nonpreferred hand.

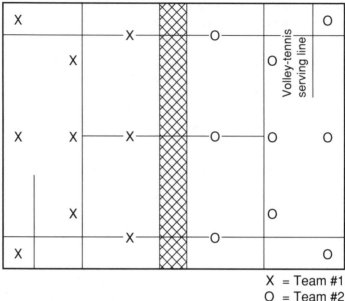

Figure 2.2   Volley-Tennis court design and nine player set-up when played on a volleyball court.

Additional Rules: Besides the standard rules from volleyball, a point or a side-out occurs for the following violations.

- The ball bounces two or more times between hits.
- The ball rebounds from the surface on one side of the court over the net to the other side of the court instead of going directly over the net after player contact.
- A player uses an overhand or sidearm serve.
- A highly skilled player spikes with the preferred hand.

Safety Considerations: Enforce spiking with the nonpreferred hand for highly skilled players, and stress that it is illogical for students to attempt to block shots because of the one-bounce rule.

Helpful Hints: Remind participants that the ball is still in play even though it might be beyond the sidelines or endline when contact is made. This is paramount, for the most effecitve spikes are angled toward the sidelines forcing opponents to move out-of-bounds for the return. Until players adjust to allowing one bounce between hits, they will contact the ball solely from the volley. To avoid this, it is often helpful initially to require that the ball be played off the bounce by at least one player before it is sent over the net. Carrying or lifting violations can be called as leniently or strictly as desired.

Adaptations for Younger Participants: Fourth and fifth graders can play Volley-Tennis successfully with the following adjustments:

- Play on a badminton court with the net level between 5 ft and 5 ft, 6 in.;
- have four players per team;
- use a medium-sized beach ball;
- set the serving line about 10 ft from the net; and
- allow players the option of throwing the ball or serving to begin each point (overhead or sidearm serves can be used).

Spasketball

Cross basketball with soccer, include a touch of team handball, and the result is a game in which players try to outscore their opponents by kicking a ball from the floor to a goal area marked on the wall for 2 points, throwing to that same goal area for 1 point, or shooting a basket for 1 point.

Objectives: Develop catching, passing, and shooting skills. Develop soccer dribbling, kicking, heading, trapping, and jumping skills. Enhance speed and agility.

Equipment: One foam soccer ball, 12 to 15 pinnies, masking tape, and four cones.

Playing Area: An indoor or outdoor basketball court. A goal area about 35 to 45 ft by 7 ft taped on a wall or fence 6 to 10 ft behind the endlines. If there is no area to define a goal, refer to Appendix A for ideas about constructing a makeshift scoring area. Two cones on the sidelines 25 to 35 ft from each endline mark the point beyond which court players are not allowed to kick or throw at the goal. Figure 2.3 shows the Spasketball court layout for two teams of 15.

Participants: One referee and 12 to 15 players per team, with a third of the players assigned to each of three positions: goalies, court players, and sideline players. The responsibilities and regulations for each position follow. If a given team doesn't have an identical number of players at each position, the other team should play with the same number per position.

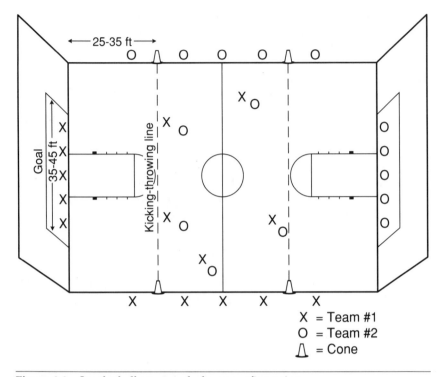

Figure 2.3   Spasketball court and player configuration.

Goalies

- protect the goal, and
- may pick the ball up with their hands and pass or kick the ball to their team's court players or sideline players while staying completely behind the endline.

Court Players

- may kick the ball from the floor into the goal area from behind the kicking-throwing line,
- may throw the ball into the goal area from behind the kicking-throwing line,
- may shoot for a basket,
- may dribble or kick the ball with their feet,
- may pass the ball with their hands, but may not dribble with their hands,
- may touch the ball with their hands or arms if it rebounds from someone's leg, foot, trunk, arms, hands, or head, but not directly from the floor, and
- may run the full length of the court without touching the sidelines.

Sideline Players

- may pick up the ball with their hands and pass or kick the ball down court,
- may run out-of-bounds with the ball, and
- may reach into the court as long as one foot remains in contact with the basketball sideline.

Game: After 5 min players rotate: goalies become the sideline players, sideline players become the court players, and so forth. Games consist of 15-min halves.

Additional Rules: Free throws are awarded for excessive contact or for being fouled in the act of shooting a basket or kicking or throwing the ball at the goal. If the ball rebounds from the wall above the top of the goal or on the side of the goal, it remains in play.

The following violations result in the ball being taken by a sideline or endline player on the opposing team who is closest to where the infraction occurred.

- A court player dribbles with his or her hands.
- A court player runs with the ball; the same stepping pattern used in basketball is permitted in Spasketball.
- Court players contact the ball with their hands when the ball rebounds directly from the floor.
- Court players kick or throw the ball at the goal while between their opponent's kicking-throwing line and the endline.
- A sideline player has both feet on the court at the same time.
- A goalie does not have both feet behind the endline.
- A player in possession of the ball fails to pass within 5 sec when closely guarded.

Safety Considerations: Stress that kicking or throwing at the goal area is illegal if the player in the offensive court is between the cones and the endline on the opponent's side of the court.

Helpful Hints: Initially, participants will not use their sideline players and goalies to their advantage. Stress that court players must get the ball as quickly as possible to their sideline players, who can roll or throw the ball to an open court player so a kick on goal can be attempted. Sideline players can be used as outlets when a court player is in danger of being called for not passing the ball when closely guarded.

The most frequent violations occur when court players use their hands to pick up the ball directly from the floor and advance with a basketball dribble. This violation occurs because participants attempt to carry over basketball skills. Besides emphasizing the differences between Spasketball and the traditional games on which it is based, provide some practice drills that require players to use their feet to lift the ball up or to pass to a teammate. Sideline players can remind court players when use of hands is not permissable and encourage them to kick the ball to their team's sideline players, who are permitted to pick up the ball directly from the floor.

Volley-Soccer

Volley-Soccer combines elements from volleyball and soccer, requiring players to send a ball over a net at tennis height so the opposing team is unable to control the ball before it rolls out of bounds.

Objectives: Develop soccer skills including drop kicking, passing, heading, dribbling, trapping, and controlling the ball.

Equipment: One leather or foam soccer ball per court. If you use defenders, 5 to 10 pinnies. Tape, chalk, or cones to mark a service line if participants are highly skilled or if playing on a volleyball court.

Playing Area: A tennis court, with the doubles sidelines serving as the lateral boundaries, or a volleyball or badminton court with the net lowered so the top is about 3 ft from the ground.

Participants: Five to 10 per team depending on the size of the court, participants' ages, skill level, and whether you use a more advanced version that includes defenders. Consult "Helpful Hints" for this variation. One referee per court. Figure 2.4 displays a seven-player set-up, six on offense and one on defense.

Game: Volley-Soccer is similar to volleyball with the following exceptions. When played on a tennis court, the serve is executed from the service line. If playing on a volleyball court, a taped line about 19 ft from the net serves as the service line. On a badminton court, either line forming the back alley can be designated as the serving line. For skilled players, the service line should be moved back farther from the net. The server may either kick, drop kick, or use a throw-in pass to send the ball to the receiving team. To be considered good, the serve must land in the forecourt, on or in front of the service line when playing on a tennis court or volleyball court. On a badminton court, the ball must hit the floor between the net and a line taped 11 ft from the net.

  The same person may make multiple consecutive contacts with the ball but they count as only one hit. If, on the other hand, person A contacts the ball, then person B, then person A again, three separate hits have been completed. Since only three separate hits are permitted, player A would need to send the ball to the opposing team.

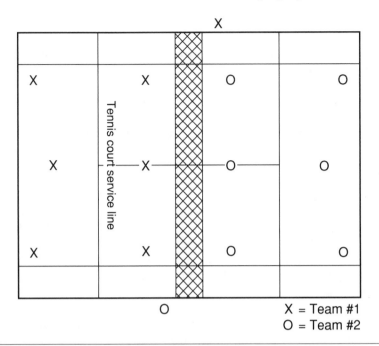

Figure 2.4 Volley-Soccer court design and player set-up for highly skilled individuals: six on offense and one on defense.

A ball must land within or on one of the boundary lines to be considered good. If the ball has touched the playing surface after the last person's contact, players are permitted to step out of the court to play the ball, provided that the contact is made with the ball in fair territory. However, if the ball is sent out-of-bounds without touching the court, a player may save the ball by sending it back on the fly either to teammates or to the opponents' half of the court. Thus, contacting a ball out-of-bounds is permitted only if the ball was sent out-of-bounds on the fly. Balls can be played from the bounce, roll, or volley, but when players return the ball over the net, it must travel from the legal playing surface of their body directly over the net.

A team can only score when serving. After a side-out, players rotate. Eleven points win the game, provided that at least a 2-point differential separates the teams.

Additional Rules: The following violations result in a side-out if a member of the serving team commits the error or a point if the receiving team does. Volleyball violations have not been listed unless there is a possibility of confusion.

- A handball occurs during a rally. A handball occurs when a player intentionally moves a hand or arm away from the body to contact the ball or gain control. Players are allowed to stop a ball by crossing their arms against their chests. During the serve, the server is allowed to hold the ball prior to kicking it to the opposing team.
- A team completes more than three hits before sending the ball over the net. If defenders are used and they contact the ball, any previous hits by the opponents are disregarded, and the count starts again.
- The ball rolls over the doubles sideline or endline after landing in the court.
- Any part of a player's body crosses the imaginary line above the net before contacting the ball.
- The serve lands outside the service area: behind the service line on the tennis court, the taped line 19 ft from the net on a volleyball court, or a line 11 ft from the net on a badminton court.
- A ball becomes trapped in the net. If the ball rolls into the net and rebounds out, it is playable provided that the three-hit rule has not been violated.
- A ball rolls under the net.
- A ball crosses the net after rebounding directly from the playing surface rather than from a legal part of the player's body.

Safety Considerations: If a player crosses an imaginary line above the net to head a ball and is kicked by a player who is trying to block the shot, severe injury could result.

Helpful Hints: When participants can control and pass the ball quickly and precisely, you can introduce added complexity by including one or two defenders, but this version of the game must be played on a tennis court. Defenders kneel by the net posts or by the net in the center of the opponent's court until a player from the receiving team contacts the ball, a player gains possession, or a second player touches the ball, depending on the skill level of the participants. Initially, it is best to play with only one defender. The defense attempts to get the ball and kick it over one of the sidelines or the baseline. Should a defender kick the ball into the net, it is a violation resulting in a side-out or point regardless of whether the ball rolls out again. Should a defender kick the ball over the net to his own team, play continues as if one of the players from the other team had returned the ball unless the ball bounces out-of-bounds, which is a violation on the defending team for a side-out or point. When there are two defenders, they should decide whether to divide the court left to right, up and back, or diagonally for guarding. To rotate using defenders, the player in the left-front position moves to defense, and the defender moves to the center-front position (if one is being used) or the right-front position.

Square Gymnastics

Square Gymnastics combines the skills of square dancing and various gymnastic stunts including rolls, scales, and stands.

Objectives: Develop static and dynamic balance within a rhythmical context. Enhance flexibility, muscular strength, and muscular endurance with appropriate gymnastic stunts.

Equipment: Seam together two standard 5 ft by 10 ft mats for each square. A record player, speakers, and fast-tempo music with a strong underlying beat, but without prerecorded calls. See Appendix A for a list of recordings.

Playing Area: A gymnasium or hard surface where mats can be placed.

Participants: Eight paired people per square, ideally one male and one female per pair. A caller, in most cases the teacher or recreational specialist.

Game: Form squares in the standard way with the female to the right of the male. Determine the head couple and number the other pairs counterclockwise. Position each couple on one side of the seamed mats. Be sure to leave a working space of at least 4 ft between partners. Ask participants to remove their shoes and stand 3 to 4 ft from the edge of the mats. Lists of possible square dance and gymnastic actions follow in Tables 2.2 and 2.3 respectively. More common gymnastic stunts, including shoulder, log, forward, backward, straddle, and dive rolls and inverted actions such as tripods, headstands, handstands, backbends, and cartwheels are also excellent choices although they are not included here. Your sequence of calls depends on the skill level of the participants. Where spotting is needed, either the partner or the corner can assist.

A typical Square Gymnastics routine:

Honor your partner

Honor your corner

Couples 1 and 3 in, and needle scale

Couples 2 and 4 in, and T-scale

All gents in and forward roll out

All ladies in and forward roll out

Swing your partner

Swing your corner

Promenade the hall

All gents in, and Chinese split; backward roll out

All ladies in, and Russian split; backward roll out

All gents in, and V-seat; back on out with a log roll

All ladies in, and front seat support; back on out with a shoulder roll

Gents in, and form a star, circle right

Ladies in, and form a star, circle left

All couples in, and forward lunge; back on out with a crabwalk

All gents in, and front seat support; back on out with a shoulder roll

All ladies in, and V-seat; back on out with a log roll

All couples in, and arabesque; back on out arm-in-arm

Do-si-do your partner

Do-si-do your corner

Couples 1 and 3 in, gents headstand, opposite lady spot that beau

Couples 2 and 4 in, gents handstand, opposite lady spot that beau

Couples 1 and 3 in, ladies headstand, opposite gent spot that gal

Couples 2 and 4 in, ladies handstand, opposite gent spot that gal

All couples in, single knee balance; and crabwalk out

Grand right and left

All couples in, and tummy balance; and back on out with a forward roll

Couples 1 and 3 in, and tripod; turn around and inchworm out

Couples 2 and 4 in, and tripod; turn around and inchworm out

Couples 1 and 3 in, gents handstand, opposite lady spot that beau

Couples 2 and 4 in, gents headstand, opposite lady spot that beau

Couples 1 and 3 in, ladies handstand, opposite gent spot that gal

Couples 2 and 4 in, ladies headstand, opposite gent spot that gal

Swing your partner

Swing your corner

Promenade the hall

Honor your partner

Honor your corner

Safety Considerations: Remind students to leave adequate working space between themselves and their partners, as well as between themselves and other couples. As a general precaution, do not have more than two people at the same time executing forward or backward rolls into the square or completing actions that require a great deal of forward momentum or balance. Instead, use backward actions or rolls done from the center of the square toward the positions on the outside of the mats.

By doing so, the four females or four males can execute stunts safely at the same time. If a person is incapable of performing a gymnastics maneuver, have that individual select a less difficult action. Be sure the spotter is informed if assistance is required.

Helpful Hints: The appropriateness of this activity hinges upon the amount of exposure participants have had to basic square dance commands and gymnastics skills and stunts.

Table 2.2   Common Dance Skills Used in Square Gymnastics

Skill	Description
Honor your partner	Bow/curtsy to the person next to you
Honor your corner	Bow/curtsy to the nearest person diagonal to you
Swing your partner	Partners are right hip to right hip, hook right elbows, turn clockwise
Swing your corner	Corners are right hip to right hip, hook right elbows, turn clockwise
Do-si-do your partner	Hands on hips, walk around your partner moving clockwise
Do-si-do your corner	Hands on hips, walk around your corner moving clockwise
Promenade	Right hand of female behind back while left hand extends in front and across gent's body; right hand of male grabs right hand of female; left hand of male grasps left hand of girl; walk around the mats counterclockwise
Circle right	All join hands and circle counterclockwise
Circle left	All join hands and circle clockwise
Grand right and left	Face partner, join right hands, walk past partner, join left hands with the next person; continue this alternating pattern until back at the starting place
Arm swing right	Partners grasp forearms with right hands and circle clockwise
Arm swing left	Partners grasp forearms with left hands and circle counterclockwise
Two-hand swing	Partners grasp both hands and circle once clockwise
Allemande left	Male faces his corner, grasps corner with a left forearm grip, circles once counterclockwise
Right-hand star	Right hands extend inward toward center at shoulder height with palm to palm and fingers pointed upward, then circle as directed
Left-hand star	Same as right hand star, but using left hands

As a rule, the gymnastic maneuvers will take more time to complete than most square dance actions. The leader must time the next call so participants can finish the skills and remain in rhythm with the music. Once participants have been successful with a standard routine, allow them to develop their own routines and demonstrate them to the others.

Table 2.3   Selected Gymnastic Skills Used in Square Gymnastics

Skill	Description
V-seat	Balance on back of derriere and bring legs and hands overhead so hands touch toes
T-scale	Balance on one leg and extend the other leg back and the upper body and arms forward to form a "T"
Needle scale	Balance on one leg, extend arms above head, flex at waist, bring head to knee, grab ankle, extend other leg so it is parallel with support leg
Stork stand	Support on one leg with the other foot raised to the inner border of the support thigh and arms extended to sides
Straddle balance	Facing forward, fully extend legs sideways, place palms on mat in front of crotch with fingers spread, raise buttocks from mat
Single knee balance	Keep one knee in contact with the mat while raising feet and extending arms toward the sides
Double knee balance	Same as single knee balance, but with both knees in contact with the mat
Jackknife	Jump up with feet together and touch hands to feet
Tummy balance	Extend arms and legs off the mat while abdomen remains in contact with the mat
Front seat support	Hands by hips, palms on mat, legs extended, raise lower body
Chinese split	Facing forward, extend one leg forward and the other leg backward while lowering crotch to mat
Russian split	Facing forward, extend legs laterally while lowering hips to the mat
Coffee grinder	Balancing on one palm and the outside of the same-side foot, walk with legs fully extended around the support arm

Creating Excitement With Nontraditional Equipment | 3

When equipment or materials not typically associated with sports becomes the focal point around which a game is developed, new activities emerge. The adage, "One person's trash is another person's treasure," certainly applies to the activities in this chapter.

Be a collector of odds and ends, if your storage facilities allow, even if you don't see an immediate use for the objects. What things should you save? Here's a short list for starters:

plastic and foam cups;

foam pellets used for packing breakable objects;

cans, bowls, or containers of varying sizes;

bottle caps;

carpet squares;

old towels;

pieces of excess material;

balloons;

broken equipment that can be handled safely;

tennis ball cans;

shuttlecock tubes;

crumpled pieces of paper and aluminum foil;

spoons;

spatulas;

wood;

rope;

string;

and the like.

The list of nontraditional items that could be used in activities is endless. More difficult than finding materials is deciding how to incorporate them in an innovative game. Let your imagination run.

Because most games involve projecting an object toward a target and/ or catching that object, you should ask how your acquired treasure can be used for those purposes. If there is no ready answer, consider whether the equipment could serve as either a boundary marker or the target. In many instances, different action patterns will be needed to execute required movements when using unusual equipment. For example, when a bottomless milk jug is used to throw a ball, overhand actions require a drastically shortened backswing to prevent the ball from dropping in back of the player.

The Games

The activities have been ordered by increasing difficulty along, for the most part, a gross-to-fine motor skill continuum. The first three games require minimal or no special skill, but, the next four require that instructors give participants practice throwing and catching using the novel equipment.

Bucket Brigade

Teams try to be the first to fill a receptacle with foam pellets or water by passing smaller containers from person to person in a line, fire-brigade-style (see Figure 3.1). No special adaptations are required, permitting players as young as third grade to participate.

Figure 3.1   Fire-brigade-style passing of containers.

Objectives: Develop cooperation and cardiorespiratory endurance.

Equipment: An ample supply of water or foam pellets. Proportionally sized receptacles for collecting and transporting the water or foam pellets (see Table 3.1). About half to two thirds of the participants on each team should have containers. They need not all be the same size, but each team must have an identical set so there is no advantage.

Table 3.1   Sizes of Containers for Filling and Transporting

Container for transporting	Container for filling
1-lb coffee can	40- to 50-gallon trash cans (4)
16-oz plastic stadium cups	20- to 25-gallon trash cans (4)
Medium-sized medicine bottles	Small waste baskets (4)
35-mm plastic film cases	Large plastic mixing bowls (4)

Playing Area: Any indoor or outdoor area that provides at least 30 yd between the full and empty large receptacles. If space is a problem, team members could assume a *U* configuration instead of being spread out in a line (see Figure 3.2). If the game is played outside, windy conditions might prohibit the use of pellets.

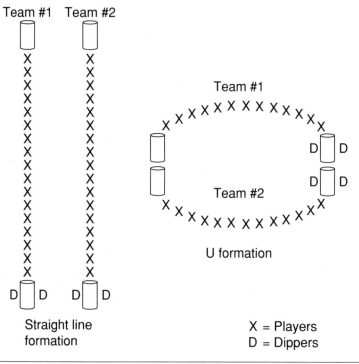

Figure 3.2   Bucket Brigade team positioning.

Participants: No more than 40 players per team. Any number of teams can be accommodated provided there is enough equipment. The supervisor observes the teams and determines which fills its receptacle first.

Game: Each team forms a line between the source of pellets or water and the empty receptacle to be filled. There should be at least 3 ft between team members. All empty containers must start at the end of the line where the foam pellet or water source is located. The two players closest to this source serve as dippers and start to fill the containers when the signal to begin is given. (A third dipper might be used with large teams; small teams might need only one, or that role could be eliminated completely.)

Once a container is filled, it is passed up the line and dumped by the last person into the empty receptacle. That individual then runs with the empty container, gives it to a dipper, and rejoins the line at that end. To keep proper spacing, participants should move closer to the emptying area as players run the containers to the dippers. The process continues until one team's receptacle has been filled to a designated level.

**Safety Considerations:**   If metal cans are used, be sure there are no sharp edges and that seams do not leak. When the game is played indoors, use foam pellets rather than water, for speed and enthusiasm will inevitably cause some spillage.

**Helpful Hints:**   As the activity progresses, more pellets or water will need to be added to the containers the dippers are drawing from. With pellets, caution the dippers not to overstuff the containers because the pellets will compress and be difficult to empty from the container; this will only slow the team down. When playing outdoors, make certain that the receptacles to be filled are on a level surface and do not leak if water is used. Another fill material that can be used is sand. If sand is used, position the teams so that it will be easy to return the sand to its original location.

Milk Jug Hockey

Participants propel a tennis or whiffle ball into a goal area by striking the ball with the sides of empty half-gallon plastic containers while bent over at the waist. Minor changes specified in "Adaptations for Younger Participants" allow children in grades 2 through 4 to play.

**Objectives:**   Develop speed and agility and reinforce striking patterns.

**Equipment:**   For a maximum of 30 participants per game, 15 pinnies, 32 half-gallon plastic jugs with the bottoms removed from four of them, a set of standard hockey goals (or six cones if a more advanced version is played), one whiffle ball or tennis ball, and masking tape to outline the goal crease areas and mark the penalty shot lines.

**Playing Area:**   An indoor basketball court is the best choice as most facilities have a wall near the endline, which serves as a natural boundary from which the ball can rebound. If there is no back wall within 20 ft in back of the goal areas, position five additional players on the endline closest to the goal their team is trying to defend. The goal crease area runs the width of the lane and is 3 to 5 ft deep, depending upon the skill of the players. A 3-ft penalty shot line is centered on the goal and 4 ft in front of it. Figure 3.3 shows the court design and player set-up for 30 players.

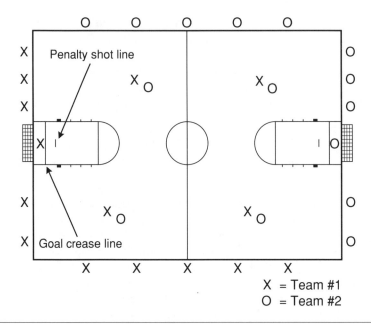

Figure 3.3   Milk Jug Hockey court layout and player set-up for 30 participants.

___

**Participants:**   One goalie, four court players, five sideline players, and an optional five endline players for each team. One or two officials.

**Game:**   Each period begins with a face-off in the center jump circle. The other court players must be positioned at least 10 ft away. For the face-off, place the ball on the court between the two opponents' jugs. Play begins at the whistle. A game consists of four 6-min periods if you use only court and sideline players, or three 8-min intervals if you include endline players. Players rotate after each period. A goal is scored when a court player or goalie hits the ball with the jug sending it into the goal, or when the ball rebounds from a part of the goalie's body through the goal. For a unique goal design that encourages more complex strategies, see "Helpful Hints."

   If you use sideline and endline players, they send the ball to one of their teammates provided they can contact it with their jug while keeping at least one foot touching their assigned boundary line. This speeds up the game by preventing the ball from rolling out-of-bounds.

   Each goalie uses two bottomless milk jugs to block or trap shots on goal, if the general skill level of the group permits students to effectively use a container in their nonpreferred hand. Goalies may also use their feet to defend the goal.

In general, most rules from the traditional game of ice hockey pertain; however, there are some exceptions.

Additional Rules: A player other than the goalie may use her or his free hand to stop the ball (if it is above waist level), but the player must immediately place the ball on the ground to continue play.

The following violations result in awarding the ball to a sideline player from the opposing team who was closest to the spot where the violation occurred.

- A court player purposefully uses his or her foot to kick or advance the ball, provided that the team retains possession of the ball or gains an advantage.
- A court or sideline player on the goalie's half of the playing area fails to touch the ball before the ball crosses the midcourt line.
- A sideline or endline player whose two feet are on the playing surface impedes play, but does not interfere with a shot on goal.
- A participant plays the ball on the face-off before the whistle has sounded.
- An offensive player enters the goal crease area.
- A defensive player enters the goal crease area, but does not attempt to stop a shot on goal. (Incidental transgression is not called.)
- A goalie leaves the goal crease area without using court player rules. While in the crease, the free hand (if a second jug is not provided) can be used to play the ball or scoop the ball into a jug; using the feet to protect the goal is also permitted.
- A sideline player hits the ball directly into the net before a court player or the goalie touches it.
- An endline or sideline player retains possession of the ball for more than 5 sec.
- A goalie retains possession of the ball for more than 5 sec while within the goal crease area.

The following transgressions result in a 1 to 3 min penalty (at the official's discretion) during which the player is removed from the game.

- Any court player exhibits repeated unnecessary roughness; no checking is permitted.
- A player's foreswing or backswing goes above shoulder level, making the jug dangerous. You might wish to enforce penalty time for this infraction after one warning. When a warning is provided, a sideline player from the opposing team puts the ball in play.

The following infractions result in a penalty shot for the player on whom the foul was committed. If it is impossible to determine which player should take the penalty shot, any court player from the opposing team can take it.

- A defensive player enters the goal crease to prevent a shot on goal.
- A player commits two or more violations requiring penalty time.

Icing is not called in Milk Jug Hockey.

Safety Considerations: Check the milk jugs before using. Occasionally, jugs with bottoms develop small cracks that could cut a person if contact is made. Take care when cutting the bottom off the goalies' jugs so no sharp edges remain. Officials need to call unnecessary roughness very strictly and stress that checking is not permitted. By encouraging the use of sidearm swinging patterns, which are the most effective means of propelling the ball, motions above shoulder level will be minimized, curtailing penalties for swings and reducing the possibility of a player being inadvertently hit in the face.

Helpful Hints: Once players learn the fundamentals of the game, a different goal design increases the possibilities for scoring. Place three cones in an equilateral triangle, with 5-ft long sides centered in the lane at either end of a basketball court. For ease of court set-up, the goal crease area is defined by the painted area in the lane. With the open-sided goal, scoring can take place from almost any position because balls that enter the goal from any side are considered good. Even if an endline player inadvertently puts the ball through the area defined by the cones, the goal is good. When playing this advanced version, goalies must use two bottomless jugs. This allows the goalie to scoop and trap shots, as well as to throw or roll the ball to a teammate, from within the lane.

Adaptations for Younger Participants: For children in second through fourth grades, eliminate the rule for advancing (where a court player kicks the ball, but his/her team retains possession) unless it results in a score, and add a fifth court player. Define the goal area as the wall in back of a basketball court with the five endline players all serving as goalies. Should the ball get past these players and roll to the wall, the point scores.

Can-Catch

Players attempt to catch a tennis ball, which has been projected very high into the air, in a trash can. Teams earn from 5 points for catching the ball on the fly to 1 point for catching it after two bounces, and the team with the most points after a set number of attempts wins. Participants as young as first grade can enjoy Can-Catch with the modifications suggested in "Adaptations for Younger Participants."

Objectives: Reinforce eye-hand coordination through striking and catching. Develop upper-body muscular endurance and teamwork.

Equipment: Four to six industrial-size, 50-gallon trash cans for a group of 24 to 36 players. Household-size, 30-gallon capacity receptacles are appropriate for grade 6. Thirty to 35 old tennis balls. For grades 6 to 9, you'll need only one tennis racket, but for older players, you'll need one tennis racket for each trash can.

Playing Area: A large field. If there is a hill overlooking the area, it is easier to project the balls with the high trajectory required.

Participants: For older players who can hit the tennis balls with the proper height, assign six players to each trash can. One player hits the balls, three attempt to catch them in the trash can, and the remaining two shag missed balls, relaying them back to the hitter. You'll need one official per trash-can team to determine if the ball was catchable and how many points each catch should be awarded. If players have difficulty hitting lofted shots, add another shagger per can and serve as the hitter yourself, or have one participant throw balls into the air on a high trajectory.

Game: Place one shagger in back of the trash-can team and the other one or two between the hitter or thrower and the trash can. Position the three players who hold the trash can so one person is on each side and the other is in the back facing the hitter. The hitter stands at least 20 to 25 yd from the trash cans. If you're using a thrower instead of a hitter, position the throwers about 15 to 20 yd in front of the catchers. To move the game along quickly and ensure that the groups won't interfere with each other, spread out the trash-can teams, and place the hitter or thrower in line with her or his team as shown in Figure 3.4.

Players must send the tennis balls high into the air to give a team ample time to judge the flight path and maneuver the trash can under the ball (see Figure 3.5). Initially, have hitters or throwers try to project the ball so teams must move no more than 5 to 10 yd for an attempted catch. It is easier to gauge a ball that will land in front of a team's position than to require that the group move backward. As players develop greater skill and confidence, the ball can be directed so players must travel farther in various directions. If you are hitting the tennis balls, send them to different teams in rapid succession. Rotate positions when a team has reached 25 points or attempted 10 catches.

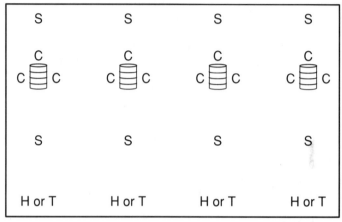

Figure 3.4   Can-Catch typical formation.

Figure 3.5   High trajectories permit catchers to maneuver the can under the ball. Communication is critical so all catchers know the direction they need to move.

Additional Rules:

- Each member of the team must have at least one hand on the trash can while maneuvering and catching the ball. If this rule is violated, no points can be scored on the attempted catch regardless of whether or not it was successful.
- If the ball is hit so it would be virtually impossible to catch, repeat the attempt.
- Players may not use their free hands or any part of their bodies to influence the flight of the ball. No points are awarded if this rule is violated.
- The first team to score 25 points wins the game, or you can compare team scores after 10 attempted catches. Teams score as follows:
  - five points if they catch the ball on the fly,
  - three points if they catch the ball after one bounce if the ball hit the can on the fly but rebounded out,
  - two points if they catch the ball after one bounce if the ball did not hit the can on the fly, and
  - one point if they catch the ball after it bounces twice on the field. (Whether the ball initially contacted the can on the fly is immaterial.)

Safety Considerations: Be sure to leave at least 15 yd between each of the trash cans, and do not leave stray balls lying on the ground. Encourage catchers to call out the direction they need to move so they can make a coordinated effort.

Helpful Hints: Commercial-size trash cans are usually available from school cafeterias. Once the ball strikes the inside of the receptacle, the team will need to incline the can backward and then forward in a rocking motion to prevent the ball from rebounding out of the can. If students have difficulty mastering this technique, crumple old newspapers into balls and cover the bottom of the can to a depth of 12 in. For improving upper body muscular endurance, you can place weights in the bottom of the garbage can, but they should be covered by at least 6 in. of crumpled newspapers.

Adaptations for Younger Participants: Children in the third grade can play a scaled-down version of Can-Catch in which only two players hold a medium-size wastebasket. Large-diameter plastic cans make good choices. You'll need to cushion metal classroom wastebaskets by crumpling newspaper into balls and lining the bottom about 10 to 12 in. deep. Position teams so that they are at the 12, 3, 6, and 9 o'clock locations with the teacher at the center. Instructors toss the balls, stressing height rather than distance. Catching the ball on the fly is worth 5 points; after one bounce, 3 points; and after the second bounce, 1 point.

Second graders can use wastebaskets also, but they will have greater success with foam balls than with tennis balls. First graders do best with a small receptacle they can hold themselves. Balloons or small beach balls are good choices for this age group because they move more slowly, allowing additional time for maneuvering the can into position to catch the balloon. Balloons are affected by the slightest breeze; thus, only indoor play is possible.

Group first graders by threes rather than by sixes, assigning one to shag, one to toss the balloon or beach ball, and one to catch it in the can. Because there will be twice as many groups, you'll need additional wastebaskets, but you'll need only two balloons for each group of three players.

Simplify scoring for first graders and second graders. For first graders, award 1 point if the player catches the balloon or beach ball before it touches the ground. For second graders, award 3 points for catching the ball on the fly and 1 point if it is caught on either one or two bounces. Adjust the cumulative point total to between 10 and 15 if it is important to declare a winner.

Milk Jug Wall Ball

Participants complete a series of throwing and catching actions using a bottomless plastic milk jug. The sequence proceeds along a difficulty continuum, and with each new skill the player must successfully demonstrate the technique one additional time. Competition takes place in pairs, and the first individual to complete the progression both forward and in reverse order is the winner. "Adaptations for Younger Participants" suggests modifications for grades 2 through 5.

Objectives: Develop eye-hand coordination and reinforce reading skills.

Equipment: For every two participants, one half-gallon or gallon plastic milk or juice container with the bottom removed, one tennis ball, one list of challenge tasks, and a piece of tape.

Playing Area: Any relatively smooth windowless wall, provided it is at least 12 ft high and there is a minimum of 25 ft of clear space in front of it.

Participants: The number of participants is dictated by the amount of available unobstructed wall space. At least 8 ft should separate each pair of players, who also serve as their own referees.

Game: Assign two players to a space near a wall where you have taped a list describing a series of tasks and provided one jug and one tennis ball. Players decide who will go first. The person who is not completing the actions reads a description of each skill to the other. For most actions, the player using the milk jug should stand at least 12 ft from the wall and hold the jug in the preferred hand. Players continue with the sequence until they make a mistake. Participants then reverse roles. When returning to the progression, players begin on the task at which they last committed an error, but start consecutive counting at one. That is, if a person made a mistake on execution 4 of task 6, when it was his or her turn again, the player would begin with the first execution of task 6. The first player to complete all the skills and redo them in reverse order is the winner. When the last task is successfully completed it does not need to be repeated; instead, the player proceeds with the next-to-last item on the list. In the following progression, simpler modifications are provided in the parentheses if skill levels dictate.

# Required	Description of the Task
1	Toss ball above head, let bounce once, and catch
2	Toss ball above head, catch on fly
3	Toss ball to wall on fly, let bounce once, and catch
4	Toss ball to wall on fly, catch on fly
5	Toss ball to wall on fly, clap hands or hit milk jug in front and in back of body, catch on fly (or after one bounce)
6	Toss ball to wall on fly, lift one leg, clap hands or hit milk jug above and below leg, catch on fly (or after one bounce)
7	Place nonpreferred hand on wall, toss ball under and over that arm, catch on fly (or after one bounce) without moving hand on the wall
8	Lift one leg, toss ball under leg to wall on fly, catch on fly (or after one bounce) (leg can be lowered after toss) (as shown in Figure 3.6)
9	Back to wall, toss ball to wall on fly, turn, catch on fly (or after one bounce)
10	Back to wall, hike ball between legs on fly to wall, turn, catch on fly (or after one bounce)
11	Toss ball to wall on fly, turn in a complete circle, catch on fly (or after one bounce)

Figure 3.6 For all tasks requiring actions between the throw and catch, the participant should have the ball contact high on the wall to provide enough time to complete the movements.

The following list indicates skills that specific grades can complete. Whichever skill is completed first must be executed successfully only once. The second skill performed is done consecutively two times, the third in the sequence is repeated three times in a row, and so forth.

Grades	Skills
6	1-7
7	3-8
8-10	3-10
11-12	4-11

Safety Considerations: Be sure there are no sharp edges after the jugs are cut. Participants might become dizzy doing task 11 if they perform the action too quickly or too many times without taking a few seconds to give their vestibular systems time to adjust. If they can alternate the directions of their turns, this inconvenience should not occur. After reading the directions for a task, players should move away from the wall so they are less likely to be hit by an errant throw.

Helpful Hints: Even though students will be informed of what is required in each of the different tasks, you should still demonstrate each of the actions before players begin the game.

Adaptations for Younger Participants: Children in the second and third grades can play this game without jugs, throwing and catching by hand. Tasks 1 through 4 on the original list are appropriate. The other tasks should be modified.

Task #	Description of the Task
1-4	Throw and catch by hand (see original list)
5	Toss ball in air, clap three times, catch on fly (or after one bounce)
6	Toss ball in air, do one jumping jack, catch ball on fly (or after one bounce)
7	Toss ball in air, hop two times, catch ball on fly (or after one bounce)
8	Toss ball to wall on fly, clap hands in front and in back of body, catch ball after one bounce

Students in grades 4 and 5 can complete the catching phase of tasks 1 through 4 on the original list while using the jug, but should toss the ball using their nonpreferred hand.

Task #	Description of the Task
5	Toss ball in air, tap jug three times, catch on fly (or after one bounce)
6	Toss ball in air, do one jumping jack, catch ball on fly or after one bounce
7	Toss ball in air, hop two times, catch ball on fly, or after one bounce
8	Toss ball in air, turn 180 degrees, catch ball on fly or after one bounce

Milk Jug Jai Alai

Players use a milk jug to throw a ball against a wall so their opponent(s) are unable to catch the ball in the jug on the fly or from a single bounce.

Objectives: Develop eye-hand coordination, speed, and agility. Doubles and cutthroat play (in which one player who serves competes against two others) require teamwork and cooperation.

Equipment: One half-gallon or gallon milk jug with the bottom removed for each player. One tennis ball per court. Tape or chalk to make lines or, for faster set-up, cones or plastic spot markers to define boundaries.

Playing Area: The court must have a solid, relatively smooth wall at least 15 ft high and a hard surface of 15 ft by 35 ft. Figure 3.7 shows the court and wall markings.

Participants: The number of players depends on the amount of available wall space; the game requires at least two players. Cutthroat requires three players, and doubles requires four.

Game: Singles, doubles, and cutthroat play generally follow the same rules as handball or racquetball; thus, only the exceptions to those rules are specified. The singles game is 11 points, and cutthroat and doubles games are 15 points. Winning requires a minimum 2-point margin.

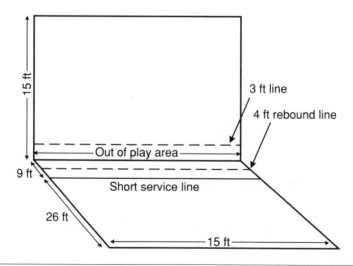

Figure 3.7   Milk Jug Jai Alai court design.

Additional Rules: These violations result in a side-out, loss of one serving hand, or a point, whichever is applicable.

- A throw fails to contact the front wall on the fly at or above the 3-ft line or rebounds before the 4-ft line running parallel to the wall.
- A player takes more than two steps after securing the ball and before throwing.
- The initial bounce occurs outside the court's boundaries, unless the opponent has made contact with the ball.
- The server fails to deliver a legal serve in one attempt. For a serve to be good, the ball must bounce in the court beyond the short service line.

Safety Considerations: Leave at least 10 ft between courts. Even so, balls that are not caught will occasionally stray onto another court. Halt the action until the ball is retrieved and replay the point if interference occurred. Trim the bottoms of the jugs carefully to avoid sharp edges.

Helpful Hints: Participants must possess some basic throwing and catching skills using milk jugs. These skills include catching on both sides of the body at various heights and throwing using underhand, overhand, and sidearm patterns. Skill levels in grades 6 and 7 might require that successful catches be permitted after a second bounce. The overhand throwing action is the most difficult to master. Many students bring their arms back too far and the ball falls out of the container. To prevent this, remind players not to hyperextend or cock their wrist as they complete the backswing.

Cupball

Participants use a plastic drinking cup to throw and catch a tennis ball while trying to score a goal. In the first variation, players aim for a basketball hoop or a hula hoop hung from the back of the iron. The second alternative has students shoot for a scaled-down soccer net, somewhat like the game of lacrosse.

Objectives: Develop throwing and catching skills, enhance agility, speed, and cardiorespiratory endurance.

Equipment: One tennis ball and 10 to 24 plastic drinking cups (16 to 24 oz) with at least 4-1/2-in. diameters (used for soft drinks at sporting events). Refer to Appendix A for additional information about where to acquire these cups. Two 24- to 30-in.-diameter hula hoops and 5 to 11 pinnies. Masking tape to outline a goal area for the lacrosse version.

Playing Area: You can use any indoor or outdoor basketball court with a wall or fence behind the backboard for both variations. Figure 3.8 shows the court design and player set-up to begin the lacrosse version on a basketball court. A large field with lines marking the sides, ends, and center of the playing area and an appropriately sized lacrosse goal can be used when playing the lacrosse version.

Participants: The basketball version requires five players per team, and the lacrosse variation 5 to 11 players per side, depending upon the size of the playing area.

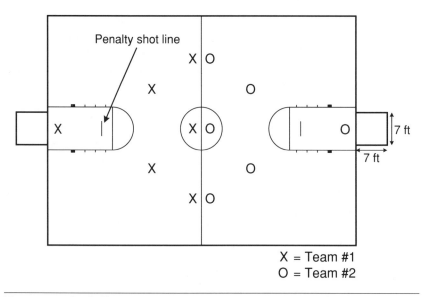

Figure 3.8   Cupball Lacrosse version. Player set-up for a basketball court with the goals taped to the walls.

Game:

Basketball Variation

Because most rules of basketball transfer to Cupball, this section specifies only those that are different. Action begins as in soccer with each team on its half of the court and one offensive player holding the ball in his or her cup. Players can advance the ball by throwing and catching or they can dribble the ball by tapping using the bottom or side of the cup. Using the free hand to play the ball while in bounds is not allowed.

Players may use their feet to stop the ball or to scoop it up into the cup, but intentionally kicking the ball is not permitted. Play continues if the ball hits any part of a player's body except as already noted. For all nonshooting violations put the ball into play at the spot of the infraction using an indirect pass. The pass must be completed within 5 sec by a member of the team that did not commit the violation, while all other players must be a minimum of 5 ft away. Players may not use their cups to knock the ball out of another player's cup. To prevent long passes downcourt after a team has scored, require at least one pass before the ball goes over the centerline. In an indoor facility use natural boundaries, allowing the ball to rebound off sidewalls or endwalls for a faster paced game. Score 3 points for a basket and 1 point for shooting the ball through the hula hoop.

Lacrosse Variation

Most rules from lacrosse carry over, but some differences apply. Players, with the exception of the goalie, are not permitted to kick the ball; however, they can use their feet to help them get the ball into the cup. The goalie is given two cups instead of one and, like the other players, is not permitted to use hands to play the ball. Take penalty throws 15 to 20 ft in front of the goal within 5 sec. Players may not use their cups to knock the ball out of another player's cup. If a few players tend to dominate the game and don't pass the ball to their teammates, make it a violation to run more than five steps before passing the ball. Where possible, use natural boundaries, allowing balls to be played off walls and curtains.

Safety Considerations: After heavy use and long periods of storage, some cups might develop small splits on the rim or along the seams. Check for cracks prior to each use to ensure player safety from cuts. Occasionally players unintentionally hit each others' hands while attempting to play the ball, but this rarely results in an injury as the sides of the cup tend to give on impact.

Helpful Hints: Players must develop some skills before participating in either version of Cupball. Teach participants to catch balls at various heights and speeds and on both the preferred and nonpreferred sides of the body. Players must be able to catch the ball from a bounce, on a fly, or while rolling. They should throw overhand, underhand, sidearm, and across the body. Using each of these actions, players should learn to pass with various trajectories and should master the bounce pass because it is a primary means for aiming at the lacrosse goal.

Towel Newcomb

Bath towels are used to propel and catch a volleyball across either a volleyball or badminton net. For less skilled players, catches from a single bounce are permitted (see Figure 3.9).

Figure 3.9   Towel Newcomb action.

Objectives: Reinforce receipt and propulsion skills and partner cooperation.

Equipment: One bath towel, approximately 26 in. by 40 in., for every two players and one volleyball or medium-size beach ball per court. Masking tape to reposition the service line. Refer to Appendix A for modifications to make throwing and catching easier.

Playing Area: A volleyball or badminton court with the net at a height of 6 ft. Move the service line to within 10 to 15 ft from the net.

Participants: Twelve per side when using a volleyball court or six to eight when playing on a badminton court. One referee per court. See Figure 3.10 for the player set-up when Towel Newcomb is played on a volleyball court.

Game: Identical rules as those used in Newcomb govern the towel version with the following exceptions, which result in a side-out or point if violated.

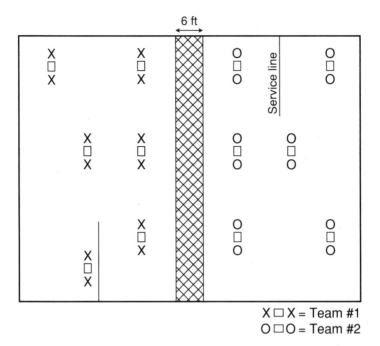

Figure 3.10   Towel Newcomb court design and player set-up on a volleyball court with team #2 serving. The receiving team should fully stretch its towels between holders while waiting to catch the ball.

- Once the ball is secured and the players have readjusted their grips on the towel, they are permitted only two steps before releasing the ball within 5 sec.
- For a play to be legal, both players must have at least one hand holding the towel, and the ball may not touch any part of a player's body except the hands before it touches the towel.
- Spiking, dinking, and blocking are not permitted.
- If you apply a one-bounce rule, each pair is allowed to legally catch the ball before it bounces twice, even when a player passes to members of the same team.
- Double catches—when the same pair catches a ball they just propelled—are illegal unless another towel touched the ball between contacts.
- Both towel holders must be in back of the service line when the ball is propelled on a serve.

Helpful Hints: Do not attempt this activity without giving players sufficient time to practice throwing and catching with the towel. Securing the ball requires giving with the contact, virtually cradling the ball in the towel. Tossing demands synchronizing the movements of the towel holders. First the pair stretches out the towel sideways with their arms lowered, and then they quickly raise their arms as the tension on the cloth increases. The angle of loft is determined by how high the partners' front hands are in relation to their back hands. The higher the back hands, the flatter the trajectory will be. To increase play among the pairs, require one pass before the team sends the ball across the net during a rally. For even more excitement, have each team serve a ball simultaneously and play until one ball is not returned. A point is awarded to the team that did not commit the violation or mistake.

Discovering New Possibilities Through Altered Actions | 4

Almost all physical activities require students to run or move without impediments and with unrestricted use of all senses. If you modify activities so players must use unfamiliar movement patterns, you'll produce innovative games.

Games that require students to play three-legged or linked forward-backward demand partner cooperation and provide locomotor challenges. Scooters can be used in standard sport units such as basketball, soccer, and the like to produce other new possibilities. Players will have to modify use of their arms or hands if they are joined at the wrists, required to hold onto one another's waist, or joined hand to hand. When you limit or eliminate vision, players must rely upon other senses to provide them with the information they need. You can drape sheets across volleyball or badminton nets or require one person in a pair to be blindfolded.

A concomitant benefit of such activities could be greater sensitivity for individuals with physical and/or perceptual handicaps. Take advantage of such teachable moments by pointing out that some of these temporary limitations simulate disabilities other people must contend with throughout their lives. However, because participants will not be familiar with these limiting conditions, be certain to stress safety.

The Games

Games requiring altered locomotion have been presented first, followed by an activity that requires participants to play in three-armed fashion.

Centipede Race

Team members coordinate their actions to move a piece of polyvinylchloride (PVC) pipe held between their thighs, on their shoulders, across their legs, and in similar ways to a designated area. This game stresses cooperative skills and demands that participants devise a strategy for effective locomotion. See "Adaptations for Younger Participants" for modifications for grades 3 through 5.

Objectives: Reinforce group cohesion and cooperation.

Equipment: Grades 6 and 7: one 10-ft section of 4-in. PVC pipe for every five to six students. Grades 8 through 12: one 10-ft section of 4-in. PVC pipe for every four to five participants. Depending upon the type of course the teams must complete, you can use cones, rope, chairs, and benches to set boundary lines or provide obstacles.

Playing Area: A large gymnasium or outdoor field. The more intricate the movement patterns, the more space must be available to maneuver the sections of pipe.

Participants: Eight sections of pipe for 32 to 48 class members. One referee if there is competition among groups.

Game: Players from one team place the pipe on or between specific body parts and try to maneuver to a designated area or through an obstacle course as shown in Figure 4.1.

Figure 4.1 Moving the centipede over the bench requires that players release the PVC tube one-at-a-time and position themselves on the other side of the obstacle.

A height disparity among players on the same team can make it difficult to position the PVC tubing. Height differences can be offset to some degree by having the participants line up in size order with the shortest person in front. Players cannot touch the pipe with their hands once the tubing is in place and the action begins unless it falls to the ground. In that case, the pipe must be repositioned, and a 10-sec penalty is assessed before the team can move. To decrease the tendency to reach down and adjust the pipe, require players to place their hands in their pockets or waistbands.

The following list includes possible actions in order of complexity. Be sure that students have success at the easier ones before progressing to the more sophisticated maneuvers.

- Moving forward in a straight line
- Moving backward
- Moving sideward
- Moving forward in a straight line, then turning around and returning to the starting position
- Weaving a figure eight through chairs or people. (Be sure to leave at least 6 to 8 ft between chairs. The closer the obstructions are to one another, the more difficult it will be to negotiate the course.)
- Transversing small obstacles such as stepping over a piece of wood, going up or down a small curb, and the like
- Passing a ball overhead from one person to another while the team is moving the pipe. (Bonus points can be awarded each time the team successfully passes the ball down the line of participants and back. Should the ball drop, movement must stop while one person retrieves it. Passing the ball then continues at the point where it had stopped.)

The following locomotor patterns can be used:

- Resting the pipe on the top of one foot
- Holding the pipe between the players' necks and shoulders (this variation requires that participants be of similar heights)
- Resting the pipe across players' ankles while they are seated with their legs extended
- Placing the pipe on players' lower backs or the backs of their knees as they lie face down
- Placing the pipe at the junction of the thigh and the trunk as players lie on their backs
- Placing the pipe between players' thighs

Safety Considerations: Check the equipment before each use to be sure it is not cracked or chipped. Tape and cushion cracks or chips as needed. Caution the participants not to throw the pipe on the ground or gym floor. If at all possible, do not use perforated tubing because the holes could chafe participants' skin. Remind players that they must judge

carefully the space required for the centipede to make turns or negotiate obstacles. If they estimate the distances incorrectly, participants at the end of the tube could hit walls or another centipede. However, the safety hazards are minimal because the groups must move slowly so they do not lose the PVC pipe. Backward maneuvers are a greater safety concern. Instruct players to look behind them so they can avoid potential impediments.

Helpful Hints: Participants will need time to devise an effective strategy for moving with the PVC piping. By allowing them to explore various options before making any suggestions, you will give them the opportunity to solve problems on their own. You can set up a series of tasks so the group works toward a goal other than finishing first. If you want to promote greater competition, you can conduct relay races or set a time goal for teams to try to best.

Adaptations for Younger Participants: Children in grades 3 through 5 can enjoy this activity by using scaled-down equipment. In grades 3 and 4, use one 8-ft section of 3-in. PVC pipe for every four to five players. Fifth graders can use the same tubing as sixth graders, but they will generally need an additional participant.

Soccer Three Ways

Traditional soccer takes on a whole new character when you couple players back to back or side by side, either requiring them to hold hands or to grasp opposite ends of a rope or cloth. Another version, which leads to interesting mobility patterns, links three participants with the middle person holding one hand of each of the other players.

Objectives: Develop kicking, dribbling, passing, and heading skills used in soccer. Enhance speed, agility, and cardiorespiratory endurance while developing partner cooperation.

Equipment: Twenty-two to 33 pinnies and 22 to 44 small pieces of cloth or clothesline if players don't want to hold each others' hands directly. A foam soccer ball for playing the back-to-back and triplet modifications, as the players' abilities to head the ball will be diminished. A regular soccer ball can be used in the side-by-side version.

Playing Area: Standard soccer field markings. Add a half circle within the goal area intersecting the endline 5 ft to the side of each post and extending 12 ft away from the endline at its widest point. Only the goalkeepers are permitted in this portion of the field. Figure 4.2 shows this court design and the player set-up for the back-to-back version.

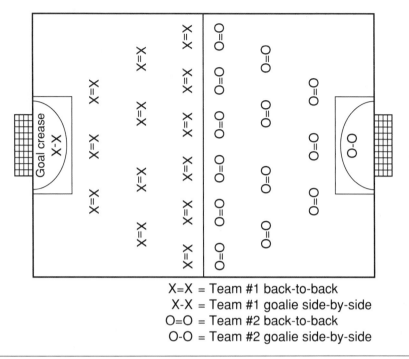

X=X = Team #1 back-to-back
X-X = Team #1 goalie side-by-side
O=O = Team #2 back-to-back
O-O = Team #2 goalie side-by-side

Figure 4.2   Back-to-Back Soccer player positioning and field set-up.

**Participants:**   Table 4.1 lists the participants for each of the three variations. The game also requires two officials.

**Game:**   Just as in regular soccer, it is critical that players stay in their general area of the field to prevent crowding. In Back-to-Back Soccer, locomotion is much easier if students face the sidelines or are on a slight angle to the sidelines and move up and down the field using sliding steps. Typical rules of soccer apply with the following exceptions.

- Only the goalkeepers are permitted in the goal crease. Incidental transgression is not called; however, repeated violations by the same defender results in a penalty kick for the opponents. If a defender attempts to block a shot, or cut off an attack angle, the opposing team also receives a penalty kick. If a shot on goal is taken from the crease, the kick is disallowed and the goalie puts the ball in play.
- If players become separated, they must link up again before they play the ball. Violation results in an indirect free kick or corner kick, depending upon where the transgression occurred. However, if the players separate immediately after a pass or a kick on goal because of the force of the kick, it is not a violation.

Table 4.1   Player Positions and Marking Patterns for Soccer Three Ways

Back-to-Back

Player position	Marking pattern
2 Wings	Right and left midfielders
1 Right forward	Left fullback
1 Left forward	Right fullback
2 Center forwards	2 Center midfielders
4 Midfielders: right, left, and 2 centers	—
3 Fullbacks: right, left, and center	—
1 Goalie: 2 people holding inner hands, playing side-by-side	—

Side-by-Side

Player position	Marking pattern
2 Wings	Right and left midfielders
1 Right forward	Left fullback
1 Left forward	Right fullback
1 Center forward	Center midfielder
3 Midfielders: right, left, and center	—
3 Fullbacks: right and left	—
1 Goalie	—

Triplet Soccer

Player position	Marking pattern
2 Wings	Right and left midfielders
1 Right forward	Left fullback
1 Left forward	Right fullback
2 Midfielders	—
2 Fullbacks	—
1 Goalie	—

- If the goalies separate while defending their goal and block a shot that would have scored, the goal counts; however, if the shot would not have resulted in a goal, the opponents are awarded a corner kick.

Safety Considerations: With the additional players, it is important for the participants to stay in their own area of the field. In Back-to-Back

Soccer, caution participants from running down the field facing the goals, which will have only limited success and could result in one person carrying another or being pulled down the field.

Helpful Hints: The focus of this game is cooperation rather than individual techniques or skill. For more advanced players, adding a second ball makes the activity more exciting and enhances the action.

Scooterized Basketball

Any activity takes on a whole new character when it can be played on scooters. Due to reduced mobility, additional players can be accommodated. You'll find changes that permit children in grades 3 through 5 to enjoy this activity in "Adaptations for Younger Participants."

Objectives: Reinforce passing, catching, dribbling, and shooting skills and improve abdominal muscle endurance. Sensitize players to the difficulties associated with handicapping conditions in which bi-pedal locomotion is not possible.

Equipment: Twelve to 20 scooters depending on whether you use full-court play or stationary forwards and guards and whether you require players to move their scooters without assistance. Pinnies for the members of one team. In grades 6 through 8, one volleyball. For grades 9 through 12, one soccer ball. Reposition the free throw line with tape.

Playing Area: An indoor basketball court with goals at the height students generally use. Move the free throw line in so that it is 6 to 10 ft from the hoop, depending on the strength and skill level of the players.

Participants: Full-court play requires six to seven people per team, all on scooters. Half court play requires five guards and five forwards on scooters. If you have a limited number of scooters and a large class, use five players on scooters per team and have additional participants help propel them. See "Helpful Hints" for other suggestions for expanding the number of participants. One referee.

Game: If you use assistants to help propel the players on scooters, the assistants can only push their partners. They can't contact the ball except on out-of-bounds plays, and they can't interfere with passes or shots. All of the rules of basketball, including rules governing dribbling, pertain with the exception of the following.

- A player travels when moving the scooter more than 2 ft without dribbling the ball.
- The following violations give the other team possession at the spot of the violation if you're not using pushers or out-of-court players

(see "Helpful Hints"). Otherwise, one of these players puts the ball in play from the closest sideline or endline.

- A player who contacts the ball when not seated on the scooter. If a player falls off the scooter when passing or shooting, it is not a violation provided the ball was released prior to slipping.
- A pusher touches the ball on the court.
- An out-of-court player has more than one foot on the court.
- A player spends more than 7 sec in the key, provided no pushers are used. With assistants, a 5-sec rule applies.

- A player who purposefully knocks another player off a scooter commits a foul, and the player who fell receives two free throws.
- Pushers who don't propel their partner carefully receive a technical foul.

Safety Considerations: Use only scooters with safety covers protecting the wheels. Be sure the scooter wheels are well oiled to prevent them from grabbing and causing the player to fall from the seat. However, be sure that the wheels are not oiled so heavily that oil drips on the floor. Caution participants to watch out for their fingers should they slip from the scooter. When you use helpers, demand that they remain in control by calling violations on them closely. If you don't use assistants, players will learn quickly that it is faster to move backward than to face in the direction they want to go. To avoid unnecessary collisions, remind students that they should look where they are planning to move when breaking clear for a pass to be certain that the path is clear.

Helpful Hints: For greater involvement, incorporate sideline and endline players similar to those used in Spasketball (see chapter 2, "Developing Hybrid Activities"). This speeds up the action, virtually eliminating out-of-bounds delays, and eliminates the need for players to assist those on the scooters.

Dribbling transfers nicely from traditional basketball, but students will need some practice with it because the rebound can bounce off to a side or between the players' legs, as shown in Figure 4.3.

Variations: Other curriculum staples, with minor modifications, can be played on scooters. These include team handball, baseball (put the fielders and the base runners on scooters and have offensive players throw the ball rather than hit it with a bat) and Newcomb (lower the net to between 4 and 5 ft). Older, more skillful players can enjoy volleyball if you use a beach ball and reduce the net height.

Adaptations for Younger Participants: For third through fifth graders, eliminate the skill of dribbling entirely, assess a traveling penalty for moving more than 5 ft while holding the ball, and use a foam soccer or

Figure 4.3   Between the legs and on the side dribbling patterns used in Scooterized Basketball. Spread the legs wide for better mobility and protection of the ball from defenders.

volleyball. Hang a 3-ft diameter hula hoop over the basket's iron bracket. For third graders, score 1 point for shots that hit the rim and 2 points for shots through the hula hoop, 5 points for a basketball field goal, and 2 points for a free throw. For grades 4 and 5, score 1 point for hula hoop shots, 2 points for free throws in the basket, and 3 points for other baskets.

Three-Armed Volleyball

Partners play volleyball side by side, holding their inside hands. Some of the rules regarding lifting and double hits are relaxed, so the game is a change of pace for players.

Objectives: Practice cooperation between partners.

Equipment: One medium-sized beach ball or foam volleyball, a volleyball or badminton net, and standards. Masking tape to reposition the serving line.

Playing Area: A standard volleyball court with the net lowered about 6 to 12 in. or a badminton court with the net raised to 6 ft. Move the serving line to within 12 to 18 ft of the net.

Participants: Use 12 players per team if playing on a volleyball court and 8 players per team if playing on a badminton court. Players grasp inner hands palm to palm to place their lower arms in a bumping position. One official oversees the action.

Game: All of the rules of volleyball apply with the following exceptions.

- Do not call double hits and carries as strictly as in regular volleyball.
- On the serve, either player may hit the ball. Requiring one person to toss while the other serves is a much more difficult skill and should only be implemented after players are able to use the self-toss successfully.
- Both partners who are serving must remain in back of the service line until the ball has been hit.
- If one partner hits the ball with either the joined or free hand and either partner contacts the ball on the next hit, it is a double-hit violation.
- If players break their grasp while playing the ball, a side-out or point results.

Safety Considerations: With twice as many players on the court, encourage the participants to call for each ball.

Helpful Hints: Players need time to practice their basic skills while joined hand to hand. The serve requires a different motor pattern. If players have developed an overhand serve, they should use it; however, if too many serves fall short or out of court, consider beginning the point by tossing the ball over the net as in Newcomb or hitting the ball underhand after one bounce. If players toss the ball, it must be projected across the net to the area bounded by the net, service line, and sidelines. Violations of this rule result in a side-out. This restriction forces participants to use high-trajectory throws, reducing the number of aces. Adding a one-bounce rule, under which a pair may legally contact the ball after one bounce following another pair's hit, will promote rallies. Using a beach ball gives participants more time to position themselves because of its slower flight speeds and higher trajectories. To allow players to have their preferred hands free for part of the game, require them to switch the hands they hold when they rotate into the left front court position.

Modifying Goals and Player Set-Up   5

You can change existing games by altering their objectives or goals. For example, permitting a team to score in two or more designated areas or by using two or more methods with each awarded a different number of points changes the action profoundly.

You can also modify games by requiring participants to aim at unusual targets. When hula hoops, carpet squares, balloons, duck pins, or bowling pins take the place of nets, goals, and basketball hoops, games take on a different nature.

Traditional sports require teams to score by propelling an object into a stationary opponent's goal. If players attempt to score points by sending projectiles toward a movable goal held by a member of the same team, nontraditional games evolve.

Modifying the configuration of players can also result in new games. The traditional favorite, dodgeball, takes on a new character when four teams form a square and aim playground balls at a large cageball rather than at their opponents. Another version results when you require participants to wend their way through a maze of opponents and back to their team without being hit below the waist.

Normally, racket activities are individual or partner sports, but when you move badminton onto a volleyball court with six players per side, a team sport emerges. You can use the same idea in table tennis. Instead of playing on a regulation surface, require teams of four to six players to hit a Ping Pong ball over a badminton net that has been lowered so that the bottom edge is about hip level.

You can use this principle systematically by applying a series of questions to the activities found in most programs.

- What other means could players use for scoring points?
- Can a different type of target be employed in this game?
- What would be the result if the goal area or target were repositioned on the playing surface?
- How can the target or goal normally used in this game be made movable?
- What other boundary or court design could be used in this activity?

- How can players' positions be modified to alter the game?
- How can a team sport be modified to become an individual or dual activity? Even more important for large classes, how can an individual or dual sport be changed into a team game?

You can use this same sequence of questions to modify the innovative games that you develop using the other five tenets identified in this book.

The Games

The activities in this chapter are ordered along a difficulty continuum from the easiest you can introduce to the more difficult. Surprisingly, the skill requirements of the participants do not coincide with this order. In fact, the most complex activity, Continuous Capture the Flag, involves the least demanding perceptual-motor skills.

Snap, Crackle, Pop

Players work in teams to dislodge or break balloons taped to a wall or fence by throwing a ball. "Adaptations for Younger Participants" specifies changes needed to allow children from third through fifth grades to play.

__Objectives:__ Develop throwing, catching, and dribbling skills along with speed, agility, and cardiorespiratory endurance.

__Equipment:__ One small playground ball or team handball; five pinnies; 30 balloons that inflate to a 9- to 12-in. sphere; masking tape; eight cones.

__Playing Area:__ The game is usually played at both ends of an indoor basketball court, but an outdoor space may be used if there is a surface at each end where the balloons can be attached. If the game is played outdoors, additional cones might be required to designate the sidelines, and more players may be needed if the playing area is larger than a basketball court. Define the goal area by placing cones 7 to 12 ft in front of the balloon surface (the distance depends on the skill and force with which players can throw the ball). Position balloons with masking tape so that there is a minimum of 3 ft between them, with the highest balloon being 6 to 7 ft above the ground and the lowest balloon about 2 ft high. Be sure to spread the balloons so they cover the entire surface. Figure 5.1 shows the court design for Snap, Crackle, Pop.

__Participants:__ Five to six participants play, depending on age and skill level. One referee controls the action.

__Game:__ Snap, Crackle, Pop is played like basketball in terms of rules and the flow of the action except as noted. Teams do not change ends of court after the half because they continue to aim at the same set of balloons. Award 3 points for balloons that are dislodged and 5 for those broken on the wall; dislodged balloons cannot be broken on the floor. Each team runs the entire court, but players cannot enter the goal area unless a balloon has been dislodged or broken and the opposing team is putting the ball into play. After a score, the ball is put into play by an opponent positioned behind the cone line. At the half, or at any time when almost all of the balloons have fallen, any balloon that was dislodged but not broken is repositioned by the referee on the wall. The game terminates either by time or when all of one team's balloons have been broken.

__Additional Rules:__ The following violations result in a member of the opposing team taking the ball out on the sideline.

- Grabbing the ball or attempting to knock it out of an opponent's grasp.

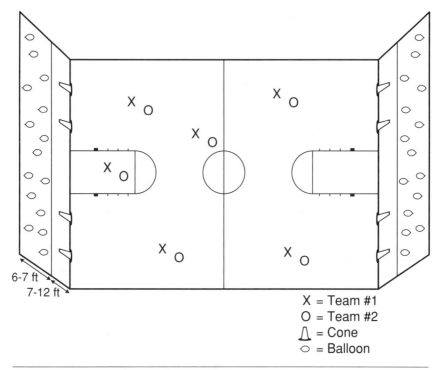

Figure 5.1   Snap, Crackle, Pop court design and player set-up.

- Entering the goal area while in the act of shooting. Should the shot dislodge or break a balloon, the score is not counted, and the balloon is not reset or replaced until the beginning of the next half.
- After a score, throwing the ball to the opposite half of the court before another player touches the ball.

The following violations result in a penalty throw. All players must be within 10 ft of the midcourt line except the shooter, who stands at the cone line. The ball is dead after the shot.

- Fouling an offensive player who was in the act of shooting.
- Entering the goal area for defensive purposes (incidental transgressions are not called if they have no effect on the play).

If a player shoots and fails to break or dislodge one of the balloons, the ball continues in play unless it goes out-of-bounds over a sideline.

Lane violations do not exist in this game.

If a ball doesn't rebound out of the goal area after a shot, a player from the team that did not touch the ball last plays the ball from the sideline closest to where the ball is located.

Safety Considerations: If participants help blow up the balloons, caution them not to put too much air into the balloon; otherwise balloons may pop in their faces. Caution helpers that forceful repeated exhalation performed too quickly can result in lightheadedness.

Helpful Hints: Have extra balloons available to replace ones broken during a violation. A variation can be played by assigning different point values to balloons of specific colors. Balloons worth more points should be positioned at the extremes of the target area to be more difficult to hit.

Adaptations for Younger Participants: For third and fourth graders, eliminate the dribbling, use larger cylindrically shaped balloons, add 10 more targets per team, use a small playground ball, and add a third scoring option, awarding 1 point if the ball hits the balloon without dislodging or breaking it. Fifth graders do not require any special modifications except for the larger cylinder-shaped balloons.

Tube Bombardment

Participants attempt to knock down a cylindrical object, such as a container in which badminton shuttlecocks are packed, by throwing or kicking foam balls at these targets. Place these objects so they can be knocked down by a direct hit or rebound from a wall, or while a defender attempts to protect the targets. See "Adaptations for Younger Participants for modifications for grades 3 through 5.

Objectives: Develop agility and fielding, throwing, catching, and kicking skills.

Equipment: One badminton tube or similar object per player. One foam soccer ball for every two to three players to ensure continuous action. Eight cones to mark the areas within which teams must place their targets. Two receptacles, such as shopping bags or boxes, to store the toppled tubes.

Playing Area: The game can be played either indoors or outdoors, even if there isn't a wall on each side of the playing area. Any space from a volleyball court to a basketball court is acceptable (larger areas are preferable for more highly skilled players). A centerline should equally divide the area and cones should be positioned as shown in Figure 5.2, which represents the dimensions of most basketball courts and is suitable for 30 high school participants.

Participants: Facility size will dictate the numbers of players. Generally 20 to 30 players can participate. One referee.

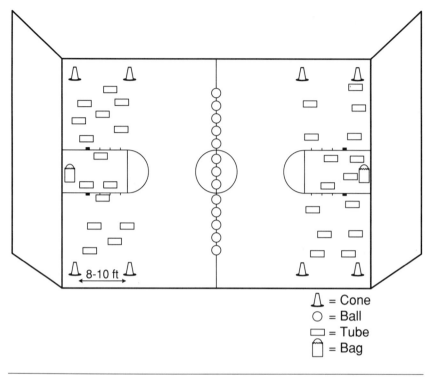

Figure 5.2   Tube Bombardment court design.

**Game:**   Each player on two equal sized teams places a tube within the coned area on the half of the court that individual will protect. Players should leave at least 3 ft between targets or a multiple knockdown might occur. Players must defend all their team's targets, not only the one they had positioned. Participants are not eliminated regardless of whether their tube has or has not been toppled.

To begin the activity, place all balls on the centerline. Players remain at the back of their half of the court touching a wall or on a designated line. At the whistle, players run forward to secure as many balls as possible for their team; however, before a ball can be put into action, it must be taken or sent back to the wall or endline. After a ball has touched this designated area, players can throw at the other team's targets. Crossing the centerline is not permitted; however, if the playing area is deep, instructors might wish to move the throwing line up so it is closer to the tubes. Should a player cross the designated throwing line and topple one or more of the tubes with the toss, no points are awarded and the targets are reset. For repeated violations, penalize the offending team by removing one of its tubes.

An inning consists of a maximum of 3 to 4 min or until all of one team's tubes have fallen. Award one point for each tube that remains standing. After completing six to eight innings, the team with the highest point total is the winner.

Safety Considerations: Fallen targets should be picked up immediately and placed in the team's box. It is very important to stress that balls must be sent back to the back wall prior to being put in play. The concern is not that a participant will get hit with a foam ball, but that a player's follow-through could hit an opposing team member in the face. This danger is significantly reduced once the game gets underway because the congestion at the centerline at the start of the action decreases when some players assume roles as defenders or shaggers.

Helpful Hints: Encourage players to loft balls, forcing an opponent to defend the targets by carefully weaving between them to avoid knocking them down. A second strategy has players aim for the wall, trying to topple the tubes on the rebound.

Occasionally, a team will purposefully curtail the action by collecting and holding many of the balls. You can impose a 15-sec rule, forcing players to send balls within their control to the opposing team's territory within that time limit. Failure to do so results in eliminating one target from the offending team.

There is little chance that a downed tube will produce an injury. However, it is in a team's best interest to remove downed tubes to prevent them from rolling into targets that remain upright.

If space is limited and/or participants reasonably skilled, have them throw with the nonpreferred hand. Kicking balls at the tubes is another alternative. For greater variety, add colored targets worth triple the number of points.

Adaptations for Younger Participants: Foam softballs can be used for players in grades 3 through 5. As a general rule, third graders need at least 28 ft of court, whereas grades 4 and 5 require 32 to 35 ft.

Mazeball

Mazeball combines a running relay with dodgeball skills, using a nontraditional player configuration for a large group of participants. Players score points by weaving through a maze of stationary opponents to a designated area and back again without being hit by a ball at or below waist level.

Objectives: Develop catching, throwing, dodging, and teamwork skills and enhance speed and agility.

Equipment: One to four foam soccer balls. Four cones to define the boundaries and an additional 4 to 10 cones to designate where the first person from each line will be positioned when they are on offense.

Playing Area: A gymnasium or any enclosed area. Although it is possible to play outdoors, a ball can roll quite a distance beyond the players who will be trying to get the runners out. The size of the teams and the skill level of the players dictate boundaries. For 30 players per team with moderate throwing and catching abilities, an area of 35 ft by 45 to 50 ft is appropriate.

Participants: Twenty to 50 per team. Two to three officials.

Game: Form two equal teams. The offensive team members form lines of four to five players each behind one of the cones on an endline. The defense spreads out over the court. With larger numbers of students, the defensive players should arrange themselves in staggered rows to cover the entire playing area. Figure 5.3 shows a court design for 30 players per team.

When playing with one ball, the first person in the middle offensive line will put the ball into play by kicking or throwing it forward so that it bounces at least once within the playing area or touches a defensive

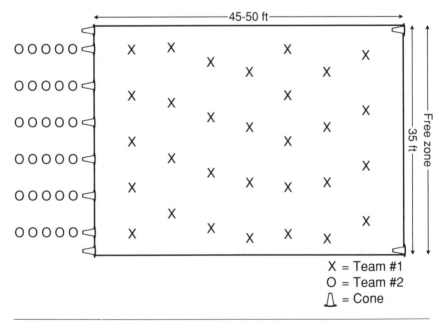

Figure 5.3   Mazeball court design and player set-up for 30 participants per team.

player. If these conditions are not met, the same player kicks or throws the ball again. This initial action is just a means of beginning play and is not an important offensive weapon. The same is true for the start of each half-inning, because the defense must complete one pass to a teammate before they can attempt to get the runners out. These requirements give the first person in each of the lines a few seconds to decide what path to take to avoid being hit. If you're using more than one ball, the one-pass rule prior to aiming at runners must be completed for each ball.

The first person in each line then runs just past the opposite endline to the free zone and back to tag the next individual in his/her line, who continues the same pattern. A point scores each time a player successfully negotiates this distance without being hit at or below the waist with the ball. Play is continuous until three runners have been thrown out. After three outs, the teams exchange places. In subsequent innings, have a member from a different line put the ball in play.

If you're using two or more balls, be sure to give them to the first person in different lines. At the start signal, each of the players that has a ball puts it in play at the same time.

A game usually consists of six to eight innings, and the team that scores the most runs is the winner. In case of a tie at the end of regulation play, complete another full inning to determine a winner.

The offense may run over any path within the playing area to elude the defense. They can change directions, go sideways, run behind defensive players, zigzag around court players, use the defensive players as a shield, and so on. The defense must work together and throw the balls to team-mates in the area the runner is approaching to increase its chance of throwing a runner out.

When a runner is hit at or below the waist, the official who observed the play should call out loudly the number of outs for the defensive team. All the referees should keep track of the number of outs by holding up the appropriate number of fingers to let the defense know how many more runners they must hit in the inning.

Being hit at or below the waist does not eliminate that person from the game. The player should run off the court toward the sides as quickly as possible. Once that person is out-of-bounds, the next player from that offensive line can begin to run, while the participant who was hit returns to the end of the line and gets ready to run again.

The official who calls the third out blows a whistle to stop the action. Before players exchange positions, the runners who scored hold up fingers to indicate the number of runs they scored personally. To be sure that each player has an equal opportunity to run during the game, have the last player who ran during the previous inning go to the end of the line when that team returns to the offense.

Additional Rules:

- A defensive player may only take one step on the court except to chase a ball that has rolled outside the playing area. When a ball rolls out-of-bounds, the closest player retrieves it. That player must run back to position before throwing the ball at a runner or to a teammate.
- Once the ball is put in play, the defensive player who gains possession may not immediately throw the ball at the runners. Rather, the player must toss the ball to a teammate on the court before it can be used to get runners out.
- A fly ball caught from the initial kick or throw is played like any other ball. This game is not like bombardment, in which the player would be considered out.
- A player must be hit at or below the waist to be out. The offensive player hit above the waist is not out and should continue attempting to score.
- A hit runner must leave the court before the next person in line can begin running. The best, and usually the fastest, method is to move off the playing area by crossing one of the sidelines. The runner who was out should then rejoin the end of the original line and wait to run again.
- After an offensive player successfully scores, she or he must tag the next person in line and then go to the end of the line and wait to run again.
- If an offensive player steps out of the field of play beyond the sidelines, that player is out.
- Runners may only remain in the free zone for 15 sec before they must leave. Should the player reenter the free zone before either scoring a point or being hit at or below the waist, the player is out. If possible, an official should give a 5-sec warning.
- Should a player be hit with the ball while in the free zone, the player is not out and play continues.
- If a defensive player violates one of the rules while in the process of hitting a runner at or below the waist, the runner is not out.
- A runner who purposefully pushes or shoves a defensive player to avoid being hit is automatically out.

Safety Considerations: Reinforce the idea that the defense should aim at the runners' legs, not above the waist. Runners can use defensive players as shields, but they can't push or shove them in the process.

Helpful Hints: With large groups, you can use two to four balls, once players understand the elements of the game, to provide greater action for both the offense and the defense and make the game more exciting.

Toppleball

The object of this fast-paced game is to knock a tetherball from the top of a volleyball standard or post by throwing another ball. See the "Adaptations for Younger Participants" for modifications for grades 3 through 5.

Objectives: Develop agility, speed, and cardiorespiratory endurance, along with throwing, catching, and dribbling skills.

Equipment: A tetherball with about 15 ft of clothesline attached serves as the ball to be toppled from a post. Thread the clothesline completely through an aluminum pole used as a volleyball standard, and tie a knot in the free end of the rope. Appendix A details the construction requirements. When the tetherball is hit from its perch, reset it by pulling on the rope. Eight to 15 pinnies and one team handball or small playground ball. If playing Toppleball outdoors, four cones and chalk.

Playing Area: Although Toppleball can be played indoors (see Figure 5.4), it is best played outdoors on a field at least 120 ft by 240 ft divided into three equal segments with symmetrical markings in the end sections and the posts positioned in the center as indicated in Figure 5.5. The middle division outdoors can be eliminated if there aren't enough players. For indoor play, use two divisions and position the standards or posts in the center of the circular portion of the basketball keys. Surround the post with a penalty circle that has a radius of 6 to 18 ft, depending upon the skill level and age of the players. Use a team handball or small playground ball to topple the tetherball from atop the post.

Participants: When played outdoors, 12 to 15 players per team, with one third of each team assigned to each division. For indoor play, eight court players per team with half assigned to each division. Two referees for indoor or outdoor play.

Game: Offensive players attempt to topple the tetherball; defensive players block shots and passes while attempting to gain control of the ball and send it to their offense. For outdoor play, middle division players work to get the ball from their defense and move it to their offensive sector. When the opposing team has the ball in the middle division, the defending team attempts to gain control and pass it to their shooters. Unlimited substitutions are permitted on a dead ball or prior to an indirect free pass, penalty throw, throw-in, or jump ball.

Two 15 to 24-min periods comprise a game. Time stops only for penalty throws or to change divisions after every two goals or after 5 to 8 min have elapsed, whichever occurs first. With three divisions, players in the central section move to the left division, while those in the left area rotate to the right division, and so on.

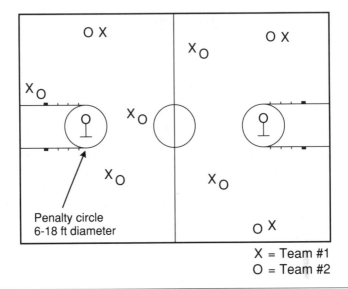

Figure 5.4   Toppleball court design for indoor play.

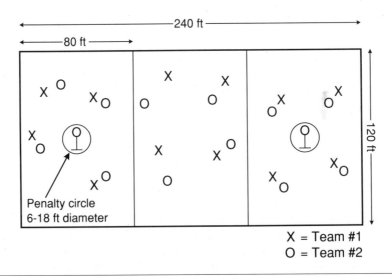

Figure 5.5   Toppleball field layout for outdoor play.

Each goal is worth 1 point. Occasionally, the tetherball will be jarred off its perch when a ball hits the metal post. This does not score; only a direct hit does. Should the tetherball inadvertently fall off the post, reset the ball by pulling the rope and let a member of the offensive team take an indirect free pass from the penalty circle (see "Additional Rules").

To begin outdoor action at the start of a half, a member of the offensive team puts the ball in play from the line separating the end and middle divisions closest to the post that team is defending. With two divisions, an offensive player puts the ball in play at the centerline. All players must be at least 5 ft from the individual who makes the initial throw.

The basic rules pertaining to movement of the ball and violations such as charging and blocking are identical to those used in basketball, and I will not review them here. However, the following definitions indicate important differences.

- Penalty shot: an unimpeded throw taken by an offensive team player at the point on the penalty circle line nearest where the violation occurred. All other players must be on the opposite half of the penalty circle. The ball is in play if the tetherball is not toppled.
- Throw-in: to pass the ball into the playing area from one of the sidelines. Any type of throwing action may be used.
- Indirect free pass: a ball put in play in any manner within 5 sec by a member of the team that did not commit the violation from the spot at which the infraction occurred or on the penalty circle, whichever is closest. Another player must touch the ball before a goal can be scored. All players must be at least 5 ft away.
- Jump ball: The same execution as basketball except the jump is taken at the spot closest to where the ball was tied up, and all other players must be at least 10 ft away. Jump balls occur when opponents tie up the ball or send the ball out-of-bounds simultaneously.

Additional Rules: The following result in an indirect free pass.

- Failure to complete an indirect free pass, throw-in, or penalty shot within 5 sec.
- Failure to pass the ball within 5 sec when closely guarded. ("Closely guarded" means the defender is within arms' distance, is between the offensive player and the opponent's goal, and has at least one hand raised to block the shot or pass.)
- Grabbing the ball out of the opponent's grasp. (It is legal to hit the ball out of the opponent's hands.)
- Entering the penalty circle. Do not call transgressions that have no influence on the action.
- Crossing into another division and influencing play, even if the player does not not foul an offensive player in the act of shooting or block a shot.
- Knocking the ball from its perch by hitting the metal post; the offensive team retains possession.
- After a goal is made, a member from the team that did not score puts the ball in play.
- During coed play a member of the opposite sex guards a player in his or her neutral or defensive division.

The following violations result in a penalty shot.

- Fouling an offensive player while in the act of shooting.
- A defender entering the penalty circle area to block a shot.
- Intentionally or repeatedly tripping, pushing, holding, blocking, or unnecessarily contacting an opponent.
- During coed play, a member of the opposite sex guarding a player in that person's offensive division while the player is in the act of shooting.

Safety Considerations: Even though no player should be within 6 to 18 ft of the pole while the ball is in play, remind participants that their movements should be controlled enough so their forward momentum does not carry them into the post.

Helpful Hints: Because the posts are positioned in the middle of the end divisions, shooting can occur from 360 degrees around the target. Having players spread out on all sides of the post is vital, because unsuccessful shots require retrieving the ball on the opposite side of the goal.

Adaptations for Younger Participants: For third and fourth graders, limit play to two divisons regardless of whether the game takes place on a basketball court or a grassy field. Eliminate dribbling, shorten the pole to 5 to 6 ft, use a medium or large beach ball as the target, and reduce the size of the penalty circle to about 6 ft. You won't be able to secure the beach ball with a rope, but since the standard is lower you can reposition the target after a score quickly. Fifth graders can aim at a large playground ball atop a 6-ft post. If younger participants have difficulty throwing a small playground ball, a medium-weight foam softball is a good substitute.

Canned Frisbee

Players throw a Frisbee into a large trash can held by a member of their own team. The movable target in the hands of a teammate provides for an exciting spin-off from the traditional game of Ultimate.

Objectives: Develop throwing, catching, agility, speed, and cardiorespiratory endurance.

Equipment: Two 25 to 30 gallon lightweight plastic trash cans, preferably with handles, are the goals. Chalk, plastic spot markers, or 24 cones to mark the goals and goal zones, one Frisbee, and 11 pinnies.

**Playing Area:**   Any large unobstructed field with minimum dimensions of

- 40 by 80 yd for grades 6 and 7 with a 7-ft goal area;
- 45 by 90 yd for grades 8 through 10 with a 6-ft goal area; and
- 50 by 100 yd for grades 11 and above with a 5-ft goal area.

Position the goal areas between 10 and 15 yd from the endlines. A goal zone, where only the goalie is permitted, surrounds the goal area. Regardless of the age of the players, the distance from one side of the goal zone to the other is 12 ft. The goal zone serves as a buffer over which the offense must project the Frisbee to score a goal. The goalie must be completely within the goal area for a score to count. A penalty throw line is 2 ft from the goal zone line. Figure 5.6 shows the court layout for grades 8 through 10.

**Participants:**   Eleven players per team: one goalie, two fullbacks, three midfielders, and five forwards.

**Game:**   Most of the general rules of soccer can be transferred to Canned Frisbee with the provision that players must use their hands to propel

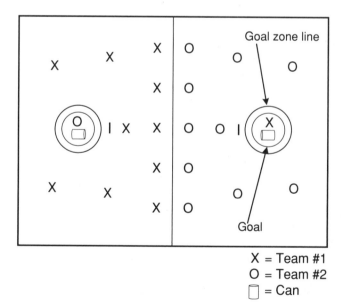

X = Team #1
O = Team #2
⬚ = Can

Figure 5.6   Canned Frisbee court design and player positioning for grades 8 through 10.

the Frisbee, and dribbling is impossible. The goalie's role is, in a sense, reversed; the goalie attempts to catch Frisbees thrown by teammates rather than to stop shots from opponents. To prevent players from running the length of the playing area while holding the Frisbee, the stepping pattern permitted in basketball is required in Canned Frisbee. Other exceptions follow.

Additional Rules: The following violations result in a free indirect pass taken by a member of the opposing team at the spot of the infraction or on the goal zone line, whichever is closest. All players must be at least 5 ft away, and the Frisbee must be thrown within 5 sec.

- A field player takes more than two steps while holding the Frisbee.
- A player intentionally kicks the Frisbee.
- A player holds the Frisbee for more than 5 sec while closely guarded. (The same definition of "closely guarded" used in basketball applies here.)
- A goalie commits a violation. See rules pertaining to goalie throws and catches.
- A player violates one of the rules pertaining to an indirect free pass.
- An offensive player other than the goalie enters the goal zone or goal area. Don't call incidental transgressions if they have no effect on the play.
- A player from one team attempts to grab the Frisbee out of an opposing player's possession, provided that player has control of the disk.
- A player makes an unsuccessful penalty throw.

Award a goalie throw when the Frisbee lands in the goal area or the goal zone. To prevent the goalie from simply handing the Frisbee to a team member and immediately have that person throw the Frisbee into the can, the offense is required to work the Frisbee to a sideline, endline, or centerline, provided that a defensive team member did not touch the Frisbee before this action was accomplished. The requirement's intent is similar to a rule used in half-court basketball where on a change of possession the ball must be taken from the sidelines or another designated spot. In Canned Frisbee, however, the offensive team retains possession if the frisbee lands in the goal area or goal zone.

The goalie is permitted to move within the goal area with the can. To score a goal, the goalie must catch the Frisbee in the can from a fly with both feet within the goal area. Neither of the goalie's hands can interfere with the Frisbee's flight. Violation of any of these stipulations negates the goal scored and results in an indirect free pass taken at any point of the goal zone line by a member of the other team.

Award a penalty throw to a member of the opposing team at the penalty throw line when any of the following infractions occur. During the throw all other players must be at least 10 yards from the goal zone line.

- A defensive player enters the goal zone or goal area to guard the goal. Don't call incidental transgressions if they did not influence the action.
- A player is called for unnecessary roughness a second time.
- An offensive player is fouled in the act of shooting.

Safety Considerations: Even though the distance from one side of the goal zone to the other is 12 ft and no one is permitted in that portion of the field except the goalie, remind participants to stay out of the area. A blind side collision with the goalie is possible and could cause serious injury.

Helpful Hints: Players should possess the basic skills of throwing and catching a Frisbee before playing Canned Frisbee. Stress that scoring can be accomplished by passing the Frisbee into the goal from virtually any position on the field. Participants tend to avoid playing behind the goal although, in fact, many shots on goal will be long. One strategy is to set up a post, or perhaps a double post, a few feet outside the goal zone line. Those players try to feed others as they cut past them for a relatively easy shot on goal. Most defense is person to person rather than a zone, which would allow a high chance of scoring if floating shots are employed.

Continuous Capture the Flag

While the overall goal of this activity is identical to the standard form of capture the flag (Smith, 1935, pp. 564-566), this altered version provides nonstop action because the flags are returned immediately by the offensive player who successfully stole the flag. Once the flag is brought back the offensive player gets a free passage back to his or her half of the field before he or she can begin offensive play again. In addition, more flags are used with point values correlated with the distance an offensive player must traverse to bring the flag across the midfield strip. The changes make scoring opportunities unlimited and conservative defensive strategies inappropriate. They result in a much more analytical game, in which players must weigh the potential of being caught with the possibility of gaining more points for their team.

Objectives: Develop speed, agility, and analytical decision making.

Equipment: Ground chalk to mark the field. Four cones to mark the corners of the playing area. Two whistles, one for each scorer. For 50 players per team, 10 passing batons, dowels, or pieces of plastic tubing each about 2 in. by 18 to 24 in. to serve as flags, including two red, four blue, and four yellow batons. One hundred pinnies or 5 ft by 6 in. strips of cloth in the following colors: 10 red or striped pinnies for the referees, 8 yellow pinnies for the jail guards and line guards, 12 blue pinnies for the roving guards, 35 green pinnies for the circle guards and offensive players from one team, and 35 royal blue pinnies for their counterparts from the opposing team. With all these colors, you might anticipate confusion, but because the referees and all of the guards from one team stay on the same half of the field, the defense can focus on players wearing either green or blue pinnies. Position designation by pinnie color allows the scorers and referees to determine if an individual is playing in the proper location.

Playing Area: Any large field free of obstructions or holes; no set dimensions. A soccer field, football field, or baseball outfield make excellent choices. These guidelines are for a playing field measuring 100 yd by 50 yd. Figure 5.7 displays the field markings and player positions for 100 participants. Refer to "Participants" for the number of players per position.

Each of the circles in which a flag is placed has a diameter of 5 ft. The front edge of the circles where yellow flags are placed should be 12 to 15 yd from the centerline. Circles for blue flags should be positioned 25 to 30 yd from the midfield line and the circles for the red flags are 40 to 43 yd from it. The circles holding yellow 1s and blue 2 flags are 10 yd from the nearest sideline. Yellow 2s and blue 1 circles are 15 yd from the nearest sideline, and the circles with the red flags are centered on the width of the field. Jails are 1 yd outside the nearest sideline and 25 yd from the endline. Each jail is designated by a 2-ft-long J marked in chalk. One cone is at each corner of the playing area. As a general rule, it will take two people about 10 min to prepare the field with the chalk circles, division lines, and the Js for the jails if they have use of a striping machine. If the field is to be lined by hand, an additional 5 min will be required.

Participants: A minimum of 25 players per team and a maximum of 50. The dimensions of the playing area and number of flags will vary with the group size. Refer to "Helpful Hints" for specific adjustments. The number of players listed in Table 5.1 for the positions is based on a team of 50.

Game: To score, an offensive player must secure a flag and completely cross the centerline to the offense's half of the field without being tagged

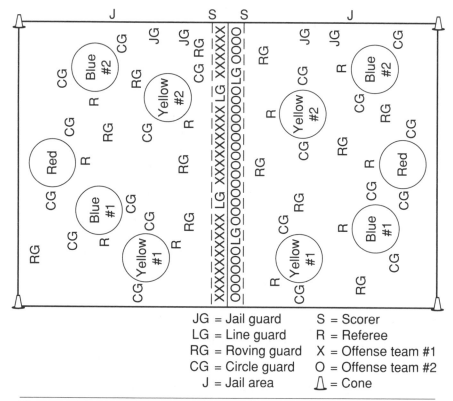

JG = Jail guard	S = Scorer
LG = Line guard	R = Referee
RG = Roving guard	X = Offense team #1
CG = Circle guard	O = Offense team #2
J = Jail area	△ = Cone

Figure 5.7 Continuous Capture the Flag field design and player positioning for 100 participants and two scorers.

by a defender. Yellow flags are worth 10 points; blue flags, 25 points; and red flags, 50 points. The team that scores the most points wins.

When tagged by defenders offensive players who are not within the circles on the opposing team's half of the field must go directly to jail after returning a flag if they are holding one. The first person in the jail must touch the J marking the prison with some part of the body. As other participants are sent to jail, they lay down and stretch out toward the centerline, keeping in contact with each other by holding onto the foot of the previous individual in line. If participants maintain direct contact, the entire jail is freed when an offensive player tags anyone in jail or when the last person in the jail can touch his or her half of the field.

At the start of each 15 to 20-min half, all players take their positions on the field. Thus, at the end of the first half, players in jails are freed. Players rotate at the beginning of the second half. Those who were guards and referees during the first half of play become offensive players in the second half and vice versa.

Table 5.1   Continuous Capture the Flag Positions and Responsibilities For 50 Players per Team

Position	Number	Responsibilities
Circle guard (CG)	10, 2 per circle	Tag opponents entering and leaving or nearing their circle
Roving guard (RG)	6	Tag opponents anywhere on the half of the field they are defending
Line guard (LG)	2	Tag opponents just as they cross or are trying to recross midfield
Jail guard (JG)	2	Tag opponents who are nearing their jail area
Referee (R)	5, 1 per circle	Judge whether or not opponents within their general area have been tagged; enforce rules
Offense (O,X)	25	Attempt to steal flags and bring them back to their half of the field; must return stolen flags; attempt to free the jail

**Additional Rules:**   The following rules apply to entering and freeing the jail.

- Players must go to the opposing team's jail under the following circumstances.
  - An offensive player holding a flag is tagged by a defending opponent before completely crossing the centerline onto the player's own half of the field. A legal tag consists of defenders touching any part of any offensive player's body with their hand(s).
  - An offensive player is tagged when her or his entire body is on the opposing team's half of the playing field and no part of it is touching or within the confines of a circle.
  - Any part of an offensive player's body goes out-of-bounds over a sideline or an endline, whether or not the player is carrying a flag. Don't call incidental transgressions by players attempting to free the jail.
  - Offensive players throw the flag to teammates; only handoffs similar to baton passes are legal.
  - Offensive players purposefully try to conceal the flag.
  - A player questions a judgment call by any referee or scorer.
  - Players show undue unintentional roughness. Intentional roughness leads to a suspension from the game.

- A player is pulled across the centerline, whether by a teammate or a member of the opposing team. The person who pulled the other player goes to jail. If the pulled player successfully brings a flag across the centerline, it is not counted in the team's point total.
- A defensive player is not positioned appropriately in the designated guarding location. Normally a person playing out of position is warned once, and the penalty is invoked thereafter. If a guard playing out of position tags a runner with a flag, that flag is automatically counted in the offensive team's point total. If the offensive player is not carrying a flag when tagged by an out-of-position guard, the offensive player gets free entry into any circle.
- There are too many guards at any designated position. No warning is given.
- An offensive player spends more than two consecutive minutes in the same opposing team's circle. The circle referee estimates the time and informs the player when there is a minimum of 30 sec before he or she must leave the circle for at least 15 sec.
- A player freed from jail fails to return to her or his own half of the field prior to rejoining play.

• Freeing the jail occurs under the following conditions.

- The line of jailed players holding onto each other becomes long enough for some part of the last jailed person's body to touch his or her team's territory. If there is a break in the jail line, none of the jailed players is free.
- An offensive player touches any part of a jailed person's body. If all jail members are touching each other, the entire jail is free. If there is a break in the jail line, only the part in which members remained in contact is released. The portion of the jail line that was not in contact when the jail was freed remains in jail. (This is similar to the concept of "electricity" used in many children's games.)

Safety Considerations: Remind players that tags should not be forceful and flags may not be thrown. Caution them not to run too close to the players in jail as their momentum might carry them into the line of jailed players. Occasionally offensive players will slide into a circle, even if they have been instructed not to do so, in an attempt to avoid being tagged by a circle guard. To assure participants' safety, instruct them in proper sliding techniques, or at least review previously learned sliding skills from softball or soccer units.

Helpful Hints: Teach older participants more sophisticated offensive and defensive strategies. Some offensive strategies might include having other team members shield the flag carrier by running alongside; confusing the defense by passing the flag among several players who are in the same circle who all leave the circle at the same time; and having flag carriers attempt to enter other circles if they are in danger of being tagged, among others. One defensive strategy is to concentrate on the flags closest to the midfield line. Red and blue flag carriers must make their way through more defensive players, and their probability of being tagged is much greater. Encourage roving guards to force flag carriers to run laterally toward the sidelines. Each sideline boundary is equivalent to a continuous line of defense because stepping out-of-bounds sends the runner to jail.

Initially, this game can be quite confusing because there is a tremendous amount of diversified action taking place at the same time. The most difficult concept for students to comprehend is that, unlike in most team activities, offensive and defensive actions occur simultaneously. Players will have an easier time understanding the game's requirements if they can see a diagram of the playing field when you review the various positions and rules.

When you initially introduce the game, limit your explanation of the rules to the most critical ones. You can present the other rules later once the basic tenets have been learned. A good idea is to stop the action after the first 5 min of play in each half on the first day you present Continuous Capture the Flag to address some of the questions that come up.

Because participants cannot assign so many different player positions, divide the group into two separate teams and have each player draw a job for the first half of play out of a hat. At the end of the first half, have each team form two facing lines, one comprised of players who had been on the offense, while the other line is made up of players who had been referees or in one of the defensive positions. The students in one line swap pinnies with the students in the other line and exchange information about their positions. Remind the participants that they will be switching ends of the field. This approach will make the transition from offense to defense most efficient. The major difficulty that arises is confusion about which of the yellow and blue flags the circle guards should defend and which flags the referees should oversee. In most cases, you can resolve the confusion quickly. One way to do so is not to change ends of the field the first day you play the game.

When there are fewer than 50 people per team, you must adjust the number of flags and the number of players at each position. Approximately half of the people on each team should play offense. To determine the number of flags to be used on one half of the field, divide the number of offensive players on one team by five, rounding upward if the answer includes a decimal of .25 or greater. Assign two circle guards and one referee per flag. Assign two thirds of the remaining players to be roving guards and split the rest of the team equally between the line and jail guard positions.

In a hypothetical example of 72 players, four flags would be used for each team of 36. Eighteen players would be on the offense and there would be eight circle guards, four flag referees, four roving guards, one line guard, and one jail guard.

Determine the distance the jail should be set back from the centerline by multiplying the number of offensive players by three. That will allow 45 to 55 percent of the offense to be held captive before the last jailed player should be able to touch her or his half of the playing field. When you use three or four flags per side, always have at least one flag worth double the number of points of the flag with the next lowest point value. These configurations are shown in Figure 5.8.

The size of the playing field and the distances from the flags to the centerline should reflect the number of participants, their skill level, and their degree of cardiorespiratory conditioning.

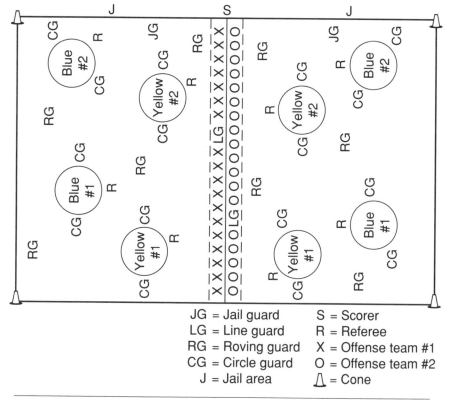

JG = Jail guard   S = Scorer
LG = Line guard   R = Referee
RG = Roving guard   X = Offense team #1
CG = Circle guard   O = Offense team #2
J = Jail area   ⌂ = Cone

Figure 5.8 Continuous Capture the Flag field design for four flags and positioning for 72 participants and one scorer.

Finding New Uses for Standard Equipment 6

We often see only one way to use a typical piece of sports equipment—the way it was originally introduced to us. But we can find new uses for standard equipment in two ways: by using it to create different movement patterns in an existing game, or by using it in a different, but well-known, activity. Games that use equipment in a different activity may at first seem to represent a hybrid innovation. Further consideration will clarify the differences, if the new activity requires that similar movement patterns and strategies be executed while using a different implement, then the activity uses a standard piece of equipment in a unique setting. However, should the game integrate rules and skills from two or more activities, the game could be logically classified as a hybrid sport.

Even though the distinction is not as clear-cut as some of the other principles we have discussed, don't be disturbed. The end result is still to increase the variety of activities for students. When you do so, you should have greater success motivating them, keeping their interest high, and piquing their curiosity. It's very satisfying when players end one activity session eager to find out what's on the agenda for the next one. Altering the use of typical equipment is one of the easiest principles for youngsters to apply, perhaps because they have less experience seeing an item employed in a set manner.

The Games

The activities have been grouped by the degree of positive transfer; one game provides for the next when considering the skills, strategies, and rules employed. Four team activities lead off the chapter. The fourth and fifth games, Team Badminton and Racket Smackit, offer some carryover to activities that use rackets or paddles. The sixth game in this portion of the book focuses on unique versions of an individual sport, golf, requiring nontraditional means for projecting the ball.

Foot-Basket

Participants attempt to score goals by shooting a football into a basketball hoop, with the obvious change of eliminating dribbling. Children as young as third grade can enjoy this activity with the suggestions in "Adaptations for Younger Participants."

Objectives: Develop skills of forward and lateral passing, catching, and shooting; enhance agility, speed, and cardiorespiratory endurance.

Equipment: One foam football appropriately sized for the players' ages and six pinnies.

Playing Area: Any indoor or outdoor basketball court.

Participants: Five or six individuals play court positions per team. One referee.

Game: All the rules of basketball pertain with the following exceptions. No dribbling is permitted, and players cannot take more than two steps before passing the ball. Nonshooting violations result in a free pass by a member of the opposing team at the spot where the infraction occurred. This pass must be thrown within 5 sec, no defensive player may be within 5 ft of the passer, and the offense can't score a goal directly from the throw. Players will make most baskets from within 7 ft of the hoop. To encourage the offense to spread out, any basket made from beyond a 7-ft radius, excluding free throws (which are worth 2 points), is worth 4 points. After a goal scores and the ball is put in play, the offense must complete at least one pass before the football crosses the centerline.

Safety Considerations: No unusual safety concerns occur in Foot-Basket.

Helpful Hints: If you want to include hiking for older players, you may do so during a free pass. The player who throws the ball on a free pass must catch it from a hike. If the player does not catch the ball from the hike, award the other team a free pass.

Adaptations for Younger Participants: For grades 3 through 5, modify the target by placing a plastic hoop over the metal portion that connects the bracket to the backboard. A 30-in. diameter hoop is appropriate for third graders, a 24-in. hoop for fourth graders, and an 18 to 20-in. hoop for fifth graders. Students score 2 points by shooting the football toward the endline and through the hoop. Sending the football through the basketball goal should be worth 4 points, and shots put through the net from over 7 ft away should be worth 6 points.

Frisbee Hockey

Players attempt to score goals by sliding a puck with a plastic bat. For older players, enhance the game's strategy by allowing scoring from the back, side, or front sections of the goal.

Objectives: Develop agility, speed, and cardiorespiratory endurance.

Equipment: Twelve to 16 plastic bats, six to eight pinnies, two standard hockey nets (or, for older players, four to eight cones), masking tape, two Frisbees, and superglue or rivets to join the flat surfaces of two Frisbees.

Playing Area: Any hard surface about the size of a basketball court; however, the Frisbees slide best on a wooden floor. Indoor facilities are preferable because the puck can rebound from natural boundaries such as the walls. Dead-end streets or parking lots are also good choices. These larger spaces can accommodate two to three additional players per team. Figure 6.1 shows the court design to play Frisbee Hockey on a 40-ft by 80-ft area with standard floor hockey goals set in about 15 ft from the endline or wall. Whether you use two cones or standard floor hockey goals to define the goal, position a 3-ft by 12-ft goal crease on each open side of the goal as seen in Figure 6.2. With this type of goal, a shot is

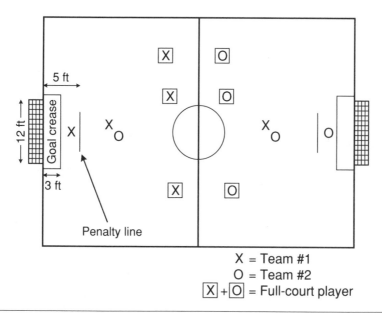

X = Team #1
O = Team #2
X + O = Full-court player

Figure 6.1   Frisbee Hockey court design using standard goals with one stationary offensive, one stationary defensive, and three full-court players.

good if it crosses between the cones from front to back or back to front. Set a 4-ft penalty line 5 ft from the front side of the goal crease and centered with the goal.

When you allow scoring from any direction, use four cones to mark a goal with 5-ft sides and a 15-ft by 15-ft goal crease area surrounding it as shown in Figure 6.3. Position a 4-ft penalty line 5 ft from the front of the edge of the goal crease nearest the centerline.

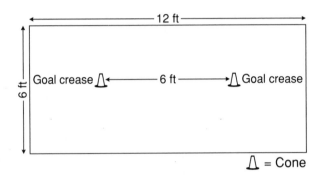

Figure 6.2 Frisbee Hockey with two-sided open goal and 3 ft × 12 ft goal crease positioned on each side.

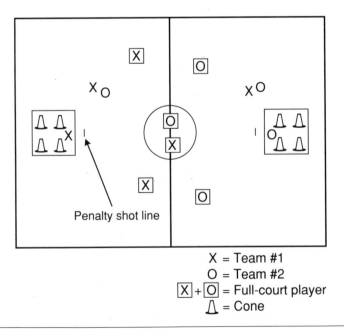

Figure 6.3 Frisbee Hockey court design and player set-up for the opening face-off when scoring in the round is permitted.

Participants: For a basketball-sized playing area, positions include one goalie, one stationary offensive player, one stationary defensive player, and three court players who are permitted to cross the centerline. With larger facilities, add one or two additional full-court players. At least one, preferably two, referees control the action.

Game: Most of the rules of ice or floor hockey pertain, with the exception of icing. This game is less violent and aggressive than other versions of hockey, with no checking or undue pushing and shoving permitted, although you should expect incidental contact. A goal scores if any portion of the puck crosses the line separating two cones within the frame of the goal or the goal mouth. Only those rules that differ from ice or floor hockey are explained here.

Additional Rules:

- Violations of the following rules result in an indirect free pass at the spot of the foul for a member of the opposing team.
  - An offensive player enters into the goal crease area. (Do not call incidental transgressions.)
  - A defensive player enters the goal crease area, but does not interfere with a shot on goal. (Do not call incidental transgressions unless they interfere with the offense.)
  - Court players advance the puck with their feet, provided their team retains possession.
  - A player raises any part of the bat above the waist on either the foreswing or the backswing. High sticking should not occur if players use sidearm actions to propel the puck.
  - A player obstructs the player in control of the puck by moving between the puck and the player who has possession of it. Players can avoid obstruction by playing opponents face to face.
  - Another player fails to contact the puck on the goalie's half of the court after a goalie throw (in which the goalie tosses the puck with the hands rather than passing with the bat). The free pass for this violation is taken at the midcourt line.
  - Players fail to execute a penalty shot within 5 sec.
- A goalie may use his or her hands, feet, or bat to defend the goal but may not purposefully lie down across the entrance of the goal between the cones. (For most shots on goal the puck will be within 1 ft of the floor.)
- The following violations result in a penalty shot.
  - A goalie lies down across the entrance of the goal.
  - A goalie steps over or cuts through the coned area marking the goal regardless of whether or not a shot on goal was executed. Goalies must go around the cones to get to the other side.
  - A defender enters the goal area and interferes with a shot on goal.

- Players must take penalty shots within 5 sec from in back of the penalty line. All other players must stay at the half-court line. Play continues if a save is made.

Safety Considerations: Remind players that they must curtail their foreswings and backswings so that no part of the bat is raised above waist level and that no player, other than the goalie, is permitted in the goal crease area.

Helpful Hints: For younger and less highly skilled players, use standard floor hockey goals. In grades 8 through 10, use two cones to mark each goal, permitting players to score with shots from the front or the back of the goal. For juniors and seniors in high school, use a goal formed from four cones to permit scoring from 360 degrees. Initially, players will not attempt shots from the back of the goal, greatly reducing the possibilities for scoring. Because goalies are required to run around the cones to defend from the other side, strategy dictates that the offense work the puck from side to side and front to back to get the goalie out of position. It is natural for the goalie to cut through the goal area. One way to reduce this problem is to attach a strip of twisted crepe paper between each of the cones. This will remind goalies of their limits while not impeding shots or tripping the goalie.

Racket Hockey

Players use tennis rackets to propel a tennis ball into a scaled-down soccer or field hockey goal.

Objectives: Develop speed, agility, cardiorespiratory endurance, and striking patterns.

Equipment: Twenty-two tennis rackets, one tennis ball or foam tennis ball, two baseball gloves (one for each goalie), and 11 pinnies. Two field hockey or soccer goals in which the scoring area has been reduced to a width of 12 to 16 ft, as marked by two cones positioned in each goal. To better define the scoring area, you can tie a 12-ft long rope between the crossbar and each cone or insert a 1 in. by 8 ft piece of wood into the opening at the pointed end of each cone.

Playing Area: A field hockey or soccer field. Add a goal crease area with a radius of 20 to 35 ft, depending upon the age and skill level of the players, from the center of the goal outward as shown in Figure 6.4. Place the penalty shot line at the apex of the goal crease line.

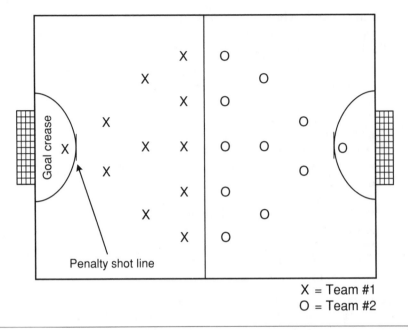

Figure 6.4 Racket Hockey field layout and player positioning.

**Participants:** Use same positions and defensive marking patterns as in soccer or field hockey: one goalie, two fullbacks, three midfielders, and five forwards. Two referees.

**Game:** Because most of the rules from field hockey carry over to the racket version, only the exceptions have been noted here. The concept of a goal crease area, in which only the goalie is permitted, is adapted from team handball. You'll find only the most common violations pertaining to this area in "Additional Rules." Because field players are not permitted to enter this portion, corners are virtually eliminated. The game expands the concept of dribbling to three options: projecting the ball along the ground in a standard field hockey dribble; bouncing the ball from the racket to the ground; and bouncing the ball from the racket into the air. Players can alternate among these three dribbling patterns at will provided they do not violate the double-dribbling rule, which prevents players from catching the ball from their own dribble and dribbling again without another player or another player's racket touching the ball.

Additional Rules:

- For the following violations, award an indirect free hit to a member of the team that did not commit the violation. This player takes the

hit at the spot where the infraction occurred or on the goal crease line, whichever is closest. All players must be at least 10 ft away and the ball must be played within 5 sec.

- A field player uses hands to pick up the ball directly from the ground. It is permissible to catch the ball on the fly directly from a racket contact.
- A field player raises the racket above shoulder height on the backswing or foreswing or to stop a ball.
- Any player takes more than two steps while holding the ball.
- A field player double dribbles, which is defined as moving the ball downfield prior to and after a legal catch without another player or another player's racket contacting the ball.
- A player catches the ball and fails to play it within 5 sec.
- A field player throws the ball to another player. Only a goalie is permitted to toss the ball, provided the goalie is within the goal crease area and is holding his or her glove and racket.
- A goalie tosses the ball while not holding a racket and glove.

• The following infractions result in a penalty hit. All other players must be located 15 yd away. The person awarded the penalty hit must contact the ball within 5 sec. If a goal is not made, a goalie hit or throw results.

- Attempting to hit the ball out of a player's hand when that individual has possession.
- Using the tennis racket in a dangerous manner or repeatedly following through above shoulder level. Usually one warning is given before a penalty shot is assessed.
- A defensive player entering the goal crease area and blocking a shot. If the defensive player enters the goal crease area but does not interfere with the play, a corner hit is taken only if that individual's team gained the advantage. Do not call incidental transgressions, as it slows the game significantly.

Safety Considerations: To avoid illegal swings, players must use sidearm patterns and follow through with a lower arc than typically used in tennis. Instruct players to step away from a player who is about to pass the ball from a self-toss. As in field hockey, players must control their actions to avoid injuries.

Helpful Hints: Air dribbling 6 in. to 12 in. upward and bounce dribbling on the ground are much more effective techniques to advance the ball downfield than dribbling the ball along the ground, for they allow the player to tip the ball up and catch it when an opponent approaches.

Team Badminton

This game merges traditional badminton with selected play and court design from volleyball. The object is to deliver a shuttle over a net in such a manner that your opponents are unable to return it over the net with no more than three contacts. For players who do not possess adequate mastery of the required badminton skills, using Ping Pong paddles and an outdoor shuttlecock reduces the complexity. Consult "Variations" for alternatives for team racket sports.

Objectives: Reinforce all the fundamental strokes used in the standard game of badminton except drives and smashes. Stress cooperation.

Equipment: Six rackets per team and two shuttlecocks per court. Four cones for each court. Tape to mark the short service line and the serving zone. For players who do not possess effective badminton skills, use Ping Pong paddles and an outdoor shuttlecock.

Playing Area: Play takes place on a volleyball court where the net height has been lowered to approximately 6 ft, 6 in. at the center. Position a short service line 6 ft from the net across the entire court. Mark the lateral boundaries of the serving zone with two 12-in. pieces of tape, placing each piece of tape perpendicular to the net, 10 ft from each sideline, with one edge touching the short serve line. To mark the forecourt from the backcourt place two cones 14 ft in back of the net aligned with each of the net poles. Figure 6.5 shows the court design and player set-up used for Team Badminton.

Participants: Six players. Extra players rotate in at the left-front position.

Game: The flow of the game melds elements from both badminton and volleyball. Serving, scoring, and rotating are similar to volleyball; however, the serve is delivered from the center-front position. Thus, 15 points is a game, there is no setting, and a team must be ahead by 2 points to win. The server may stroke the shuttle anywhere across the net as long as it lands in the forecourt, within the area bounded by the sidelines, the short service line, and the imaginary line between the cones. Birds cannot be served consecutively to the same frontline player (use the lines that define the service zone to gauge which third of the court the shuttle falls in). Frontline players are not permitted to contact shuttles when standing in the rear portion of the court; likewise, backcourt players can't cross into the forecourt to play the bird. However, backline players can hit a bird that has not crossed the cone line as long as they are standing

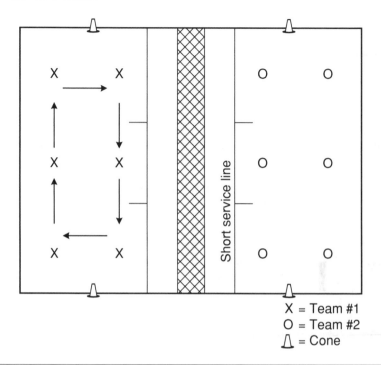

Figure 6.5   Team Badminton court layout with a clockwise rotation like that used in volleyball.

within the rear portion of the playing area. A similar rule applies to the frontline players. As long as they are in the fore-half of the court, they can contact a shuttle that has already crossed into the backcourt. After the serve, each team must return the bird to the opposing team with no more than three and no fewer than two player contacts. This requires members of the same team to work together so one player can't dominate the match.

Additional Rules: Because most of the rules of badminton apply directly to Team Badminton, they will not be reiterated unless there could be potential confusion caused by different volleyball rules. The following violations are exceptions. They result in a side-out if the serving team commits the violation or a point if the receiving team is in error.

- A backcourt player hits the shuttle while positioned in the forecourt, or a forecourt player hits the shuttle in the backcourt.
- The server delivers two consecutive serves to one of the forecourt locations.
- The server delivers the serve to the opponent's backcourt.

- During a rally, teammates fail to use a minimum of two or exceed a maximum of three player contacts before they return the shuttle to the opponents.
- A player tries to block an opponent's shot by intentionally holding the racket just above net level when the opponent hits the shuttle.
- A player from one team hits the shuttle twice in succession.

Safety Considerations: Individuals must talk to each other and call for the shuttle to ensure that a frontcourt and a backcourt player do not attempt to contact the shuttle simultaneously. Encouraging backcourt players to position themselves within 7 ft of the baseline and frontline players to locate themselves within 2 to 3 ft of the short service line decreases the chance of two players interfering with each other.

Variations: The team concept can be generalized to other racket sports with some minor adjustments. These new games not only provide novel experiences, but also demand a lower level of skill. A brief outline of each of these alternatives follows.

Team Ping Pong

Team Ping Pong uses an identical court set-up to Team Badminton. It requires one Ping Pong paddle per participant and one table tennis ball per court. For less highly skilled players, you can substitute a small beach ball. The object is to hit the ball over the net so the opposing team is unable to return it before the ball has bounced twice in their court. No smashes are permitted. Team Badminton rules apply with the following exceptions.

Additional Rules:

- The server must let the ball bounce once before contacting the ball with a paddle held below waist and wrist level.
- On the return of serve, the receiver must let the ball bounce once.
- During a rally, players may contact the ball on the fly or after a single bounce.
- The ball must travel over the net from a direct paddle contact rather than rebounding across the net from the floor.

Team Tennis

Team Tennis requires four players per team, each with a racquetball racket, shortened tennis racket, or Ping Pong paddle and one foam tennis ball per tennis court. Divide the court into four rectangles as shown in Figure 6.6, with the doubles sidelines serving as the lateral boundaries. Adjust the

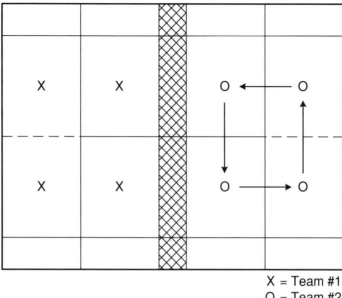

Figure 6.6   Team Tennis court design and player configuration with counterclockwise rotation. Forecourt players defend the area bounded by the doubles sideline, net, centerline, and long service line. Backcourt players each defend half of the rear portion of the court.

serving line in accordance with the strength and skill of the players in relationship to the equipment used. The ball must bounce before being served underhand, and no smashes are permitted. The ball must also bounce prior to the initial contact on the return of serve. Consult Volley-Tennis in chapter 2, "Developing Hybrid Activities," for additional rules.

Team Pickleball

The same court design used in Team Tennis applies to Team Pickleball with the addition of a nonvolley-zone line 6 ft from the net parallel to the tennis service line. The game requires six players per team, each with a pickleball paddle, and one pickleball per court. It uses the same rules as Team Tennis; however, players are not permitted to contact the ball on the fly while standing in the nonvolley zone. Thus, the ball must bounce prior to contact if the hitter is located within 6 ft of the net.

Helpful Hints: When deciding whether or not Team Badminton is an appropriate activity, assess the players' level of badminton skill rather than their age or grade level. Students should be able to demonstrate

adequate mastery of the basic skills of underhand clear or any type of service motion, overhead clear, overhand drop, and net drop so they can participate successfully. Initially, the playing area will seem a bit crowded; however, the lateral area a player must defend is a similar size to that required in the traditional game of badminton doubles when a side-by-side strategy is employed.

In all the team racket activities, backcourt players have an easier time judging whether the ball or shuttlecock will enter their portion of the court. Hence, they should take the initiative in calling the shots.

Prior to beginning play, have players practice passing the shuttle, foam tennis ball, or pickleball to one another while in their positions on the court. Stress that the game requires passes with high trajectories to allow teammates time to move to the appropriate position. Generally, crosscourt passes are more effective and easier to adjust to than birds or balls directed at players located immediately in front of or in back of the player hitting the shuttle or ball. A good strategy is for players to try to return the shuttle or ball deep into the opponents' court.

Racket Smackit

Baseball and softball take on a new dimension when batters use a tennis or racquetball racket to propel a tennis ball.

Objectives: Develop throwing, striking, and catching skills and enhance speed.

Equipment: One tennis or racquetball racket, one tennis or racquetball ball, and a set of bases. If you will use pitching, chalk to mark off a special strike zone.

Playing Area: A softball field with the bases moved back to 75 to 90 ft for grades 9 to 12, unless batters are required to hit pitched balls or with the nonpreferred hand. If you use pitching, position a 3 ft by 4 ft rectangular strike zone so that the 3-ft side nearest the batter is 3 ft in front of and centered on home plate if playing with a tennis racket or 2 ft in front of home plate if playing with a racquetball racket.

Participants: Ten to 12 players can be accommodated per team by positioning up to 6 in the outfield. At least one, but preferably two, umpires.

Game: Standard softball rules apply, except for the requirements of batting and striking out. If you use pitching, the pitcher must lob the ball underhand, and it must bounce within the strike zone if balls and strikes are to be counted. For faster play, have batters hit a self-toss, either before

or after the bounce. For very skilled players who could consistently out-hit the dimensions of the field, use a tennis ball and racquetball racket or have players bat with the nonpreferred hand using a tennis racket and tennis ball. A batter strikes out when two strikes occur any way possible, including a foul ball for the second strike.

**Safety Considerations:**   The umpire should make sure that the tennis racket does not interfere with a play at the plate. If you permit sliding, instruct players in proper technique. Remind the players at first base that they should play on the inside of the bag to avoid collisions with the runners.

**Helpful Hints:**   In Racket Smackit, players will be able to send the ball on much deeper and higher trajectories than when playing softball. Thus, some outfielders will need to play much deeper than usual and must rely on teammates to relay the ball to the infield.

Golf Three Ways

Each of these versions of golf is a spin-off from Frisbee golf, which was introduced by Fluegelman (1976). The object is to hit a designated object, which serves as the cup, in as few strokes as possible. However, rather than using traditional golf equipment, these games use other means of projecting a ball. Consult "Adaptations for Younger Participants" for changes required for children in the third and fourth grades.

**Objectives:**   Fungo and tennis versions develop eye-hand coordination. Aerobic golf improves cardiorespiratory endurance and throwing skills. Each activity reinforces some basic mathematical operations.

**Equipment:**   A minimum of one tennis racket or one plastic whiffle-ball bat per two players for the tennis and fungo versions respectively. A different colored foam tennis ball and an index card to record scores for each participant. A pencil or pen for each group. For aerobic golf, each participant needs a stopwatch or a watch with a timing function and one different colored foam tennis ball.

**Playing Area:**   Any large outdoor area. The space need not be completely free of obstructions, but the obstacles should not impede the ball's flight.

**Participants:**   The number of players depends upon the size of the playing area. The grounds surrounding most suburban or rural schools should permit 30 to 40 individuals to participate at the same time.

Game: Assign groups of two to four players to a general location. Determine an initial tee-off order. The first person surveys the environment and plans out the hole. For example, the first player in line might decide to start at this tree, go around the right side of the street lamp, go up the hill around the left side of the bush, and hole out by hitting the no parking sign.

Fungo and Tennis Versions

Once all know how the hole is to be played, begin action following the standard rules of golf for the fungo and tennis versions. Participants toss the ball and try to make contact with their bat or racket. Each swing counts as one stroke regardless of whether or not it connects with the ball. Once each individual in the group has planned a hole, the order repeats.

Aerobic Golf

Aerobic Golf uses a similar set-up as just described; however, players throw their tennis balls rather than strike them, and each player starts a stopwatch upon tee-off and stops the watch upon holing out. To prevent players from getting too close to each other during play, stagger starts by 20 to 30 sec. Players keep track of their own strokes and time. After all group members have holed out, use the time of the player who finished most quickly as the benchmark to compare others in the group. For each additional 5 sec, add one half of a penalty stroke to the player's score for that hole. Do not count any deficits less than an entire 5-sec unit. For example, if the finishing times are 1:35, 1:48, and 1:33 for players X, Y, and Z respectively, then player's Z's time is the reference point. Player X doesn't receive any penalty, as there is only a 2-sec difference between player X and player Z. Player Y must add 1-1/2 strokes to her or his total, as there is a 15-sec difference from player Z's time. In the rare event that two balls land close together and the players arrive at their balls simultaneously, the person who caught up to the player who teed-off earlier has the right of way.

Safety Considerations: The use of regulation softballs and bats or even standard tennis balls would be ill-advised. Ideally, this activity takes place in a natural setting; however, many schools are not surrounded by appropriate terrain and the risk of an errant ball hitting a person or breaking something is not worthwhile. Participants should not devise holes that require them to cross streets unless they can be blocked off to traffic.

Helpful Hints: The first time you present this activity, encourage players to create simple layouts that most players should be able to complete in six to eight strokes per hole. For additional variety, striking actions rather than throwing patterns can be used in Aerobic Golf, but players will need to have their own plastic bats or tennis rackets.

Adaptations for Younger Participants: Children in grades 3 and 4 can play a modified version of fungo or tennis golf by throwing balls instead of hitting them on simple predesigned holes outlined on index cards each group carries with them. For example:

- Tee-off at second base, finish by hitting the gym exit door.
- Tee-off at soccer goal near parking lot, finish by hitting the backstop.
- Tee-off by water fountain, finish by hitting nearest tennis net post.
- Tee-off by equipment shed, finish by hitting home plate.

With descriptions on index cards, you can provide different sequences of holes by reordering the cards. If scoring is important, put a pen or pencil at the end of each hole.

If fifth graders have difficulty hitting fungo style, they could hit the ball as it rests on the ground. If so, shorter holes must be designed.

Shared Tennis, Badminton, or Ping Pong

Doubles play becomes a truly shared experience when players alternate hitting using only one racket. All racket sports that do not require a safety thong worn around the wrist can be played in this fashion.

Objectives: Develop the same skills as in the traditional versions of tennis, badminton, and Ping Pong. Enhance cooperation between partners.

Equipment: One racket for every two players, and three tennis balls or slow-flight shuttlecocks or one table tennis ball per foursome.

Participants: Two players per team.

Playing Area: Standard facilities for the specific racket sport.

Game: Play progresses as in the original game, with the exception that after one person on a doubles team takes a stroke, that player must get the racket to her or his partner quickly so the partner can send the ball or shuttle over the net. Players can exchange the racket most effectively by handing it, rather than tossing it, to the teammate.

Safety Considerations: The player who is waiting for the racket should be sure that he or she does not crowd his or her partner while that individual is stroking. Players should hand their rackets rather than toss them.

**Helpful Hints:** This activity is geared for players who possess at least an intermediate skill level in the original sport. As a whole, most students in the eighth grade or above could successfully play Shared Badminton and Ping Pong. Increased court coverage in tennis makes this game a better choice for students in grades 11 and 12, although a double-bounce rule would allow students as young as sixth grade to play. Younger and less highly skilled players will find it easier to play the tennis version with a shortie tennis racket or a racquetball racket without wearing the thong.

In badminton, most exchanges should take place as near to the home position as possible, while in tennis, hand-offs should occur near the center of the baseline. These positions will place the next hitter in the most advantageous area to return the shot. With the close proximity of players in table tennis, the location for paddle exchanges is not as crucial. At the same time the racket switch is being made, the player who just contacted the ball or shuttle must move out of the way. Initially, players will forget about the need to get the racket to a partner and will be late in the hand-off. Have students think "switch hit," which represents the sequence of actions after a contact. Use standard strategy for each sport, but remember that racket exchanges away from the ideal place put the receiving team at a distinct advantage.

Wall Ping Pong

The object is to hit a table tennis ball, racquetball, or tennis ball with a Ping Pong paddle so the ball hits the playing surface and bounces from a wall into the opponent's area such that it cannot be returned prior to a second bounce.

**Objectives:** Develop striking skills and agility.

**Equipment:** One table tennis paddle for every player. One Ping Pong ball, racquetball, or tennis ball for each group of competitors for indoor play or one racquetball or tennis ball for outdoor play. Masking tape or chalk to mark the boundaries.

**Playing Area:** The court requires a relatively smooth wall at least 5 ft high. The number of people playing against each other determines the width of the court. For each participant, a 6-ft span of wall is needed to define the court the individual will defend. The depth of the playing area from the backline to the base of the wall is 6 to 8 ft for either indoor or outdoor competition. See Figure 6.7 for the design of a court for three competitors.

**Participants:** A maximum of four players in a single game.

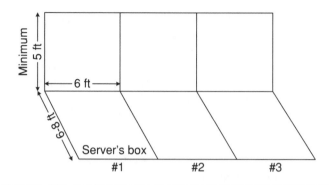

Figure 6.7   Wall Ping Pong court design for three players.

**Game:**   The following general rules pertain regardless of whether there are two, three, or four players competing on the same court. Violations result in a side-out or point.

- Participants must hit the ball so it bounces once on the floor or ground before rebounding off the wall and bouncing into one of the opponent's boxes. Should the ball carom beyond the court boundaries after hitting the wall, the play is illegal.
- The same player may not contact the ball twice in succession.
- Players must return the ball after one bounce in their box.
- When serving, the player must be located in the leftmost box and must contact the ball after it rebounds from a single bounce in her or his own area.
- Only the person who is serving earns points.
- Participants may have only one foot in their designated area of the court.
- Players use an unbiased method to determine initial positioning in the boxes.

**Additional Rules:**   The following rules apply when two competitors are playing.

- If the server is unable to return the ball to the opponent in the proper manner, the players exchange boxes.
- A game consists of 15, and a player must win by a minimum of 2 points.

With three or four competitors, other rules apply.

- The game is 11 points, but a 2-point minimum lead is not required.
- If the server is unable to return a shot properly, he or she loses the serve and moves to the court at the far right. All other players move

one box to the left. Thus, the person who was immediately adjacent to the server now takes over that individual's playing area and becomes the new server. This shifting can be seen in Figure 6.8.

- If one of the other players is unable to return a ball, that individual moves to the far right playing area, while the remaining two participants move one box to the left. The server in this case would not move because she or he did not commit an error. For example, if the boxes are numbered 1 to 4 from left to right and the player in space 3 fails to return a ball properly to an opponent, player number 3 would move into space 4 and the player in space 4 would then defend the third box. The server and player number 2 would not move. This rotation is shown in Figure 6.9.
- It does not matter where players 2 through 4 hit the ball as long as they do not step into a box they are not currently defending. In essence, they are working together to hit the ball into the server's area so they can dethrone that person, occupy that box, and score points.

Safety Considerations: Occasionally, contact between paddles occurs, but this is more of a finesse game than one that demands powerful hits and the chance of an injury is quite small. Regardless, encourage players to call for their shots.

Helpful Hints: Players should be able to demonstrate forehand and backhand strokes before competing. Initially, students will hit the ball directly to the wall rather than using a downward and outward striking motion to send the ball to the playing surface. If students have played table tennis, the same striking pattern used on the serve in that sport is

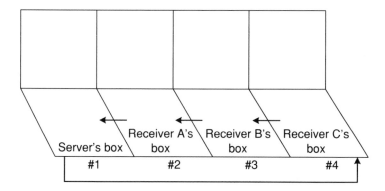

Figure 6.8 Rotation pattern in three- or four-player Wall Ping Pong when the server loses the serve. The person in box #1 goes to box #4 and all other players shift one box to the left.

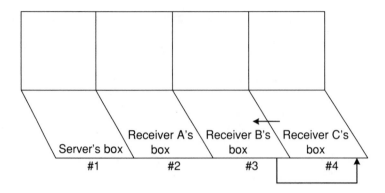

Figure 6.9   Rotation pattern in three- or four-player Wall Ping Pong when the person in box #3 commits an error. The players in boxes #1 and #2 do not change places. Players in boxes #3 and #4 switch positions.

used for each stroke in Wall Ping Pong, with the head of the paddle pointing sideways rather than downward. Fast reflexes and good judgment using principles from geometry and physics will help players determine the angles of incidence and rebound required to send the ball into the area desired.

Providing Multimedia Adaptations | 7

A world of possibilities exists for developing innovative games rooted in ideas found in television, video games, pinball, and board games.

Television

Contestant-type game shows provide a natural setting that, modified to some degree, can produce activities popular with adolescents. The major change for most programs is incorporating physical activity. Probably the easiest and most direct way to do this is through relay races. The team that completes the relay first gets to answer a question, choose a letter, earn a piece to the puzzle—whatever is appropriate to the game. Even though the relay provides the basic element for movement, participants will perceive the games as different provided the ultimate goal varies.

Other television programming can give rise to novel activities. For example, action stories can provide the basis for activity, with players imitating the movements of fictitious characters.

Murder mysteries are solved by correct interpretation of a series of clues through deductive reasoning; this concept provides the foundation for Treasure Hunt. This game requires that participants perform physical activity after they decipher a coded message. The information in one clue leads a team to another clue, followed by another, and so on, and eventually to a reward or treasure.

Video and Pinball Games

The recent rage in home entertainment has been video games, a technological spin-off from pinball machines. The themes common to these computerized wonders are no different from most games played on the court or in the gym: Score more points than your opponent, eclipse your personal record, complete a task within a given time frame, or render your opponent helpless before she or he forces you into the same state. It is simply the context in which these goals are achieved that makes them appear unique. That is the essence of what you must try to capitalize on: By transferring context from the screen to the playground, you can create a seemingly novel activity.

It is usually impossible to translate every aspect displayed by the video or pinball game. Focus instead on carrying over the major theme—lack of predictability and the possibility of losing control of the object that is the primary vehicle for scoring points. To achieve this, modify selected areas to adapt the game to your setting.

Recreational Board Games

Recreational board games modified to fit within a gymnasium setting provide another means for developing innovative games. For example, take the idea behind the game of Battleship, which is to sink the enemy's craft before its forces can destroy your own. You can use tin cans as the targets and balls for torpedoes or missile shells. To enhance the element of suspense, restrict the players' vision by draping sheets over nets at badminton height.

The critical element for transposing ideas from board, video, or pinball games or from television game shows into an activity that includes movement is an open mind that asks, "How can the basic premise of this show or game be adapted to a physical setting?" By using and thinking about the examples of activities in this section, you should gain greater insight into how to succeed in creating your own games.

The Games

The games in this chapter have been ordered according to the degree of physical conditioning incorporated into the activity. With the exception of "Beat the Clock," each places a moderate to extensive demand on cognitive elements such as recalling facts and rules, spelling or using word associations, abstract reasoning, and understanding mathematical concepts.

Human Anagrams

Participants spell answers to questions about rules, terminology, history, strategy, and the like in sports or in other knowledge areas. The game provides an excellent medium for reviewing information and is superb for rainy days.

Objectives: Reinforce selected cognitive information and spelling skills.

Equipment: Two to four letter sets made by printing letters on old file folders cut in half. Use large bold strokes and print letters on both sides of the folder. To help distinguish one team's alphabet from another, draw each set of letters using a different color marker. The letters *J, Q, X,* and *Z* are not used very often and you might not want to include them. To differentiate the letter M from a W, place a line under the letters so that they look like M and W respectively. One cone for each team, one whistle, and a list of correct answers for each judge.

Playing Area: When two teams are competing, Human Anagrams requires approximately 60 ft by 18 ft unless you use one of the modifications suggested in "Helpful Hints." Play generally occurs indoors because participants will be seated at times; however, a grassy or hard outdoor surface is also appropriate.

Participants: If you use all letters except *J, Q, X,* and *Z,* 18 to 22 individuals can play per team; however, you might want to eliminate some other letters if there are not enough players to comprise two teams. Each team should have its own judge if possible.

Game: Divide the class into at least two groups and assign each team a captain. A team should not have more than 22 or fewer than 18 players. With fewer than 18 per team, too many participants will be responsible for two letters, which can be very confusing even for older players. If a player must be in charge of two letters, assign letters that don't occur very often in the same word, such as *V* and *K, W* and *P, C* and *B,* or *H* and *F.* Never put one student in charge of both a consonant and a vowel or two vowels. Avoid double letters by eliminating some letters that you would otherwise use. If you use this strategy, select the letters that occur infrequently. Good choices would be *F* and *V,* or perhaps the *K.*

Have the captain of each team give one or two letters to each team member. Vowels and other letters that are used a great deal should be given to the better spellers. The configuration for two teams is shown in Figure 7.1.

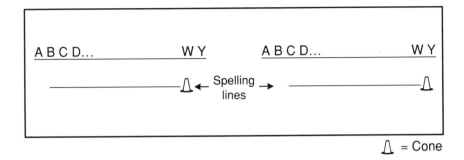

Figure 7.1   Human Anagrams design of playing area and team positioning for two teams.

Players should line up so their letters spell the alphabet properly from left to right. If a participant is assigned two letters, that person should sit in the spot for the letter that occurs first in the alphabet. It is not necessary to leave gaps where the missing letters would normally be found.

After the leader asks a question, the players with the letters that spell the answer get up, move to the spelling line, and stand in proper order to spell the word, holding their letters facing their teammates. After the participants are in the proper position and have physically spelled the answer, they must shout out their letters in consecutive order to spell the word verbally. The players then sit down on the spelling line to signal that they are finished unless a judge is assigned to each team, in which case the judge blows a whistle to indicate that the team has completed its physical and verbal spelling. The first team finished receives a point if the word is spelled correctly both physically and verbally. The team with the greatest number of points is the winner.

When players form their answer, they must do so in a manner that permits the rest of their teammates to read it properly, not backward. Sometimes a player will hold a letter upside down or sideways while physically spelling the word. This is treated as an error. Teammates can tell the player to correct the problem, but if the errant letter has been spelled out verbally, the entire word must be spelled aloud again after the correction is made. Encourage players to look over the top of the file folder to be sure their letter is positioned properly. Participants assigned two letters occasionally will display the wrong one. Again, this error must be corrected before the team has successfully spelled the answer.

If the same letter appears twice in the answer, it's called a jumping letter. The individual with that letter must physically move when spelling the word. Initially, the person should line up at the position in the word where the letter first appears. Once the player shouts the letter aloud in

its first position, he or she must move to the spot where the letter appears next and say it again. If one person has two letters and the answer demands that both appear, the player should follow the same rules for jumping letters. But the player with two letters must interchange the file folders so that the correct letter is shown in its proper place in the word. Changing places with a jumping letter can be seen in Figure 7.2.

Each judge makes certain that the participants have positioned their letters correctly, gives the signal to begin spelling the word aloud, and makes sure players have spelled their word properly. When these requirements are met the judge blows the whistle, informing the leader and players that the round is over. With judges, the spellers don't have to sit down after they have shouted out their letters. Each judge must be given a list of answers.

If only two teams are competing and no judges are available, instructors should ask a question and then stand even with the team members who will not be spelling out the solution. From that vantage point, it should be possible to see and hear the words being spelled, provided the other members of the team are quiet.

Safety Considerations: No unique safety concerns occur with Human Anagrams.

Helpful Hints: Gear the complexity of the answers to be spelled to the participants' cognitive development. If you want to add more physical

Figure 7.2   Human Anagrams word formation with a repeated letter changing positions.

activity, require participants to do some type of exercise in a designated area prior to moving to the spelling line. Have players do 20 jumping jacks, 10 squat thrusts, or 15 sit-ups (provide mats). Require them to skip, run, or hop to the opposite side of the gym or to do similar activities. Another possibility is to leave the letters spread in order on the floor across the gym. If a letter is required in the answer, the player must retrieve it before going to the spelling line. The only drawback to these modifications is that they require a larger playing area.

To be certain that all the letters of the alphabet are used a number of times throughout the activity, plan the questions carefully. An easy way to use all the letters is to use answers that demand five or more different letters. Preplanning will also help you assign pairs of letters to one player if needed.

Be sure to play a few practice rounds with short responses so participants understand what they must accomplish. In these trials, include at least two examples of words with repeating letters. If you will accept abbreviations or shortened versions of an answer, such as NY for New York or VB for volleyball (the periods have been deleted as punctuation marks are not used in Human Anagrams), make that clear when introducing the game. Keep in mind that acronyms and abbreviations will involve fewer players at one time. However, more questions could be presented in a given activity session. If a solution calls for an answer using two or more words, inform the teams prior to posing the question.

Wheel of Fortune

Standard relay races take on a new twist when the reward for finishing first allows the team to choose a letter so members can guess a secret phrase or the name of a famous person, place, or thing. See "Adaptations for Younger Participants" for modifications for grades 4 and 5.

Objectives: The nature of the relay dictates the essential elements being developed. Reinforce word formulation, word recognition, and spelling.

Equipment: Equipment depends upon the actions in the relays. One cone per team, computerized fanfold paper or butcher's paper, tape, and a wide-tipped magic marker. A stopwatch or watch with a stopwatch function.

Playing Area: Ample space for the relays and a wall, which serves as the game board to attach the paper containing the spaces where the message will be filled in.

Participants: Teams consist of four to six people, with space dictating how many can play. One judge to help determine the order of finish in each relay.

Game: Participants should be informed of what category the message they are trying to guess represents: a famous person, a thing, a phrase, a place, a title, and so on. The team that finishes the relay first is given 5 sec to select a consonant. Should that letter appear in the message, the appropriate blank spaces are filled in. That team then has 5 sec to provide an answer. If any other team's members know the answer, they should not reveal it for no guess is permitted until a team has placed first in one of the relays. Teams can choose vowels when the first place team beats the second place team by more than a certain number of seconds, when the same team places first in two consecutive relays, or when a special round is designated.

Safety Considerations: Specific safety concerns depend on the actions required in the relay; however, you must provide a large enough area between the teams' positions and the wall where you fill in the message to permit participants to decelerate without hitting the wall.

Helpful Hints: Letter guesses that don't appear in any of the words should be posted on a separate piece of paper. Since teams will be fairly close together, remind them to whisper among themselves so others do not gain an advantage. If the game is proceeding too slowly because of inappropriate guesses, allow teams to select two consonants at a time. Older players are adept at figuring out puzzles representing famous people, and these also make good choices for participants in the lower grade levels. Students seem to be more challenged by deciphering phrases containing a number of words. Be sure to print large letters so the teams at the ends can easily see them.

Adaptations for Younger Participants: Make the phrases to solve concrete and offer a general hint to help narrow the category. For example, if the word were *gymnasium*, instead of saying that it is a place, provide a hint by adding that this place is very active. Or, if the word is *string bean*, specify that this is a thing that is green. Such assistance will reduce the abstractedness of participants' guesses.

Dominoes, Cards, and Letter Pick-Up

Players work in groups of two or three in relay fashion to secure dominoes, playing cards, or letters of the alphabet, one at a time, to meet a goal.

Objectives: Develop speed and agility, while reinforcing solutions of number and word problems.

Equipment: For every 24 to 36 participants, six sets of dominoes each containing 36 tiles; four sets of playing cards or enough Go Fish, Old Maid, or Crazy Eight sets to equal approximately 200 cards; or three sets of letters in the same proportions as used in the board game Scrabble. These letters can be printed on unruled index cards cut in half. If you want to assign letters varying point values, consult one of the commercially available word-building games to determine the points. Twelve to 20 traffic cones to designate team positioning.

Playing Area: A hard surface or a gym floor. Play could occur on a field, but windy conditions might preclude using playing or index cards. A basketball court comfortably services up to 20 separate teams of two or three players each.

Participants: Twenty-four to 60 participants. The supervisor or an assistant as a judge.

Game: Position an equal number of two- to three-player teams on each of the endlines of a basketball court. Cones or markers help participants remain in the area they have been assigned. All materials to be used in the game should be spread out face down along the centerline. To prevent students from remembering where a particular object is located, divide into teams after participants distribute the items. Once players are at their stations and have decided an order for retrieval, pose a problem and explain any constraints that must be followed. At the whistle the first person brings back one item and places it in front of the cone. Then the next person does the same, and the pattern continues until the team has successfully reached a solution. When a team has reached the maximum number of items it may have in its possession, the next player must bring one item back to the center and leave it face down before selecting another to bring back. Players may not turn objects over at the centerline in an attempt to get the one their team needs; the first object touched must be taken. The game continues until first through third places are determined, and 3, 2, and 1 points are awarded respectively. The proper solution can be verified by an assistant, another team, or a supervisor. After each round, teams return items to the centerline, distributing them face down among the other items. Periodically, rotate teams one or two stations to prevent members from remembering where objects have been placed.

The complexity of the problems must depend upon the cognitive development of the participants, and each problem must have many solutions. If not, there might not be enough items so each team has the opportunity to complete the task. If there are only four possible solutions, for example to find an ace of hearts with over 200 cards to select from, the round might take a long time to complete. Examples of typical problems follow.

Dominoes

- With no more than four dominoes in your possession, the sum of the spots must equal 28 to 31.

- Retrieve two doubles (each domino half has the same number of spots).
- With no more than five dominoes in your possession, form a connected string linking four together.
- With no more than four dominoes, form a sequence ("straight") so that the number of spots on three separate dominoes is consecutive, for example, 6, 7, and 8 or 10, 11, and 12. The strategy is quite complex, for dominoes that total 2, 3, 11, and 12 spots can only be formed one way, whereas other numbers can be reached by different combinations. A domino that totals 5, for example could be a 4-1, or a 2-3 combination. Even college students do not realize this at first!
- With no more than 3 dominoes in your possession, the sum of the spots should total the number of football players on the field while a play is being run.
- Retrieve a domino that will answer:
    - the number of innings in a regulation baseball game
    - the number of balls for a walk
    - the number of points for a touchdown
    - the square root of 25
    - the number of players on the basketball court at one time

Cards

A similar game can be developed with playing cards. Philosophically, some school districts might not approve of using playing cards. Crazy Eight cards work just as well. Some possibilities for this game follow.

- Retrieve one card of each suit.
- Collect four cards of the same suit.
- Gather two red or two black picture cards.
- Form a five card straight with no more than six cards in your possession.

Letters

- With no more than six letters in your possession, form a five-letter word.
- Collect three different vowels.
- With no more than six letters in your possession form a five-letter word that is a given part of speech, such as a noun, adverb, or verb.
- Spell out the answer to a given question with no more than seven letters at your station. For example, provide a skill or stroke used in swimming, a word associated with baseball, or the last name of a member of the nearest professional football team. Again, remember that the problem must have multiple solutions.

Safety Considerations: Remind students to slow down prior to approaching the materials near the centerline to avoid stepping on the tiles or cards and possibly slipping.

Helpful Hints: You can make the rounds last longer by requiring teams to solve two problems at the same time, perhaps one using dominoes and another using cards. For example, with no more than three dominoes in your possession, link them together, add up the number of spots on the dominoes, and collect no more than five cards that equal the spot total on the dominoes. Or, using no more than eight letters, form a number word between 2 and 10, then collect two playing cards that add up to that number.

Treasure Hunt

Small groups work together to decipher a series of clues that will lead them to a treasure hidden before the start of the game. Each clue requires participants to complete an activity and tells players where their next clue is located. The first team to get to the treasure by solving all of the clues correctly gets to share the bounty. Consult "Adaptations for Younger Participants" to use Treasure Hunt with second, third, and fourth graders.

Objectives: Qualities fostered depend on the activities you specify in the clues. Enhance cardiorespiratory endurance or speed (or both) if players must travel long distances between clues. Reinforce logical thought processes, word manipulation, spelling, and math.

Equipment: For each group—two pencils, four to six sheets of paper on which the clues will be placed, envelopes marked with the clue number and the team's name (e.g., Red #1), one set of clues, and two sheets of scratch paper. If the clues do not require extensive deciphering, scratch paper and pencils may be optional. The treasure can consist of anything you choose, such as candy, cookies, raisins, extra playtime, and so forth.

Playing Area: Any large space where participants can be supervised; however, it is best to play outdoors where players will be able to move freely from one place to another. Most outside environments around a school or community recreation center provide excellent locations for placing clues, including a water fountain, backstop, net post, a base or home plate, basketball post, flagpole, soccer net, front and back doors, and so on.

Participants: Five to eight members per group. At least one less team than the number of clues. At least one recreational specialist, and preferably at least one assistant to hide the clues, supervise the activity, offer hints if groups are stymied, and determine if the clues have been properly decoded.

Game: Treasure Hunt is an excellent warm-up activity, or it can be used as a change-of-pace in a conditioning unit. The function of the game depends upon the actions or skills you require participants to complete.

Clues are cryptic messages devised ahead of time and placed in envelopes with the clue number and the team name printed on the outside. The envelopes are then placed in the appropriate location, with the exception of the first clue for each team. That clue is handed to the captain; each remaining clue can be hidden in a specified general location, or placed in a prominent spot for teams to recover. When teams do not have to spend a long time searching for where a clue has been hidden, the activity progresses more quickly with greater emphasis on deciphering the message, completing the required actions, and moving from location to location.

Clue codes are the key to this event. If the clue read, "Each person shoot and sink two lay-ups then go to water fountain," the type of code and actual message could appear in the many different ways that follow.

Mixed-Up Spelling With Words in Proper Order

HAEC NPRESO TOSOH NAD KINS OTW Y-ULASP DNA
OG OT RAWTE OFTANIUN

Mixed-Up Words

PERSON WATER AND SINK GO EACH TO AND
FOUNTAIN LAY-UPS TWO SHOOT

Pictures

Alphabet Represented by Numbers
1 = *A*, 2 = *B*, 3 = *C* . . . 26 = *Z*

5-1-3-8   16-5-18-19-15-14   19-8-15-15-20   1-14-4   19-9-14-11
20-23-15   12-1-25-21-16-19   1-14-4   7-15   20-15   23-1-20-5-18
6-15-21-14-20-1-9-14
(Note: Hyphens between the numbers differentiate one letter from the next.)

Alphabet Represented by Numbers
26 = *A*, 25 = *B*, 24 = *C* . . . 1 = *Z*

22-26-24-19   11-22-9-8-12-13   8-19-12-12-7   26-13-23   8-18-13-16
7-4-12   15-26-2-6-11-8   26-13-23   20-12   7-12   4-26-7-22-9
21-12-6-13-7- 26-18-13

Vowels Represented by Numbers
1 = *A*, 2 = *E*, 3 = *I*, 4 = *O*, 5 = *U*, and 6 = *Y*

2-1-C-H   P-2-R-S-4-N   S-H-4-4-T   1-N-D   S-3-N-K   T-W-4
L-1-6-5-P-S   1-N-D   G-4   T-4   W-1-T-2-R   F-4-5-N-T-1-3-N

Use of Math to Determine Number Words in the Clue

Each person shoot and sink (Figure Math) lay-ups and go to water fountain

    20 + number of runs a grand slam scores

    + number of balls in a walk

    − number of points a lay-up in basketball is worth

    × number of outs in one full inning of baseball

    − number of yards in a half of a football field

    − number of eggs in a half dozen

    ÷ by the number of players on the court for one basketball team

    × the number of infielders in softball

    ÷ by the total number of points of a field goal and a safety in football

    ÷ by the number of sides in an octagon

Adding Extraneous Repetitive Letters (e.g., OP)

EOP-AOP-COP-HOP   POP-EOP-ROP-SOP-OOP-NOP
SOP-HOP-OOP-OOP-TOP   AOP-NOP-DOP   SOP-IOP-NOP-KOP
TOP-WOP-OOP   LOP-AOP-YOP-UOP-POP-SOP   AOP-NOP-DOP
GOP-OOP   TOP-OOP   WOP-AOP-TOP-EOP-ROP
FOP-OOP-UOP-NOP-TOP-AOP-IOP-NOP

Abstraction for Part of the Clue (e.g., indicated by capital letters)

Each Person BANG and Sink II Lay-ups and Go to the SLURPING PLACE

You can use any combination of these types of clues. Other possibilities are limited only by your imagination and creativity.

Normally, each game requires between five and eight different clues. The clues are identical for each group, but the order in which the teams complete them is different. The last clue must be the same for all teams as it leads them to the treasure. Table 7.1 presents a sequence of seven clues for five teams.

Clue 1 is handed to each team to begin the Treasure Hunt. Clue A for the Red Team directs them to a particular area where the Red Team's second clue (Clue B) is hidden. When Clue B is deciphered, it instructs the Red Team players to go to a specific area to find Clue C, which represents the Red Team's third clue, and so on.

The clues are ordered consecutively for each team regardless of where they direct the team to move. This means that Clue A = Clue 1 for the Red Team. Clue B = Clue 1 for the Blue Team. Clue B = Clue 2 for the Red Team. Clue C = Clue 2 for the Blue Team, and so on. By numbering the clues and putting the team's name on the outside of the envelope, you'll be sure the groups solve their clues in a specific order.

It helps to write the location where you *intend* to hide the team's clue under the flap of the envelope so you or an assistant don't get confused. For example, if Red Clue 1 (which you handed to the team captain) deciphered to "Two push-ups then go to the tennis net," you would have to hide Red Clue 2 at the tennis net. Thus, under the flap of the envelope with Red Clue 2 you would write *Tennis Net* since that is where you would hide that envelope. Following this logic, say that Red Clue 2 decoded to "Jog around the tennis courts four times, then go to the bleachers." Red Clue 3 would be placed in the bleachers, and under this envelope flap you would write the word *Bleachers*. In other words, *you*

Table 7.1   Ordering Seven Clues for Five Teams

Team name	#1	#2	#3	#4	#5	#6	#7
Red	A	B	C	D	E	F	G
Blue	B	C	D	E	F	A	G
Green	C	D	E	F	A	B	G
Orange	D	E	F	A	B	C	G
White	E	F	A	B	C	D	G

hide the next clue where the previous clue directs the team to go. This is crucial, for if the sequence is not correct, some or perhaps all of the teams will not be able to complete their Treasure Hunt.

Additional Rules: The following rules apply:

- A team must decipher the clue and complete the actions before they can go on to the next clue.
- A team must complete all clues in the proper sequence.
- The first team to find the treasure, or a promissory note for one, is the winner, provided they have correctly deciphered each of the clues. Once a team finds the treasure, they must not disturb it. They must give the instructor their clue sheets to verify that they have properly decoded the messages.
- If a team has worked for 3 min to decipher a clue and still cannot break the code, the supervisor can provide a hint. However, a team may receive a maximum of four hints during the entire activity.
- Other teams' clues may not be disturbed.
- A team can't begin to work on a clue until all its members have arrived at the site where the clue is hidden.
- A team caught violating any of the rules can be penalized at the discretion of the leader. The team members might be required to do a specific activity before they can proceed or remain seated for a set period of time. You can also disqualify the group, depending on the infraction.

Safety Considerations: As a whole, this activity includes no unusual safety concerns. The actions players must complete might require that certain warnings be given, however.

Helpful Hints: To keep the activity level as continuous as possible, hide the clues so players don't have to spend a great deal of time searching for the envelope once they reach the proper location. Be sure the team's name and clue number are visible so other teams' clues will not be taken by mistake.

The first time you play this game, limit the number of clues to four, even if there will be two teams using the same sequence for their clues. Once you successfully conduct a Treasure Hunt on a small scale, you will understand the pattern that must be followed so the game runs smoothly. For a better conditioning effect, develop a sequence of clues that requires participants to traverse relatively long distances between them.

Keep track of the elapsed time between when the first and second teams find the treasure. If the first team committed an error in deciphering the clues, you can give them that specific amount of time—the number of minutes between when they finished the Treasure Hunt and when the second team finished—to solve the problem. If the members of the first team can't correct the difficulty in this allotted period, and the second team's clues have been appropriately decoded, the second team would be declared the winner. Thus, it is important to stress that decoded clues must be written in the proper form on the actual clue sheets in the envelopes. This will allow you to check the solutions very quickly.

Adaptations for Younger Participants: For younger children who have only limited reading and abstract thinking capabilities, eliminate the need for deciphering by writing simple descriptions of the required actions and the location of the next clue. You could also cut out or draw a picture of the activity the participants will perform at each station. You could place a snapshot or hand-drawn picture in the envelope to let the team know where they will find the next clue. Fifth graders do not require any special modifications, but you should use relatively simple codes with them.

Beat the Clock

Teams try to complete a series of challenge tasks in a given period of time to earn points. Beat the Clock has two different methods of awarding points. In the "all or none" method, the team that achieves the goal gains the points. A second, more effective, alternative allots points based upon the degree to which the team was able to meet the objective. This reward structure based on a sliding scale is more appealing than the pass/fail approach of standard relays. For either version, you'll need to collect some data from participants for the actions and skills you will use to devise challenging, but realistically attainable, objectives.

Objectives: Depend upon the tasks to be performed. The example that follows develops selected skills in basketball, soccer, and volleyball; upper body and abdominal muscular endurance; agility; and speed.

Equipment: Depends upon the tasks players will perform. For 10 stations: five jump ropes, one eraser, two mats, one volleyball, one soccer ball, one 5- to 8-lb medicine ball, one basketball, 16 cones, and a stop watch. At each station, tape an index card explaining the requirements and point scale. A piece of paper and a pencil for each team to record the scores.

Playing Area: While this activity can take place outdoors, an indoor area the size of a basketball court offers possibilities for many more activities. Figure 7.3 shows the layout for 10 separate stations.

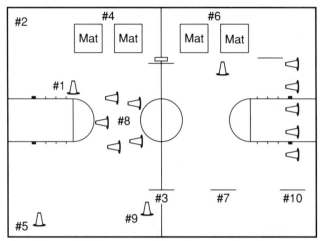

= Cone; Station action—1 = Lay-up; 2 = Jump rope; 3 = Eraser put & take; 4 = Sit-ups; 5 = Volleyball wall pass; 6 = push-ups; 7 = Skipping relay; 8 = Medicine ball pass; 9 = Soccer ball wall pass; 10 = Basketball dribble.

Figure 7.3   Beat the Clock station positioning.

Participants: Teams of four to six. Assign each team to a separate station to begin the activity.

Game: Students complete activities at different stations, spending 1 to 1-1/2 min at each. Decide beforehand on the time limit and be consistent because players will rotate to the other stations. The following example outlines activities for five-member teams of eighth graders, using 1-1/2-min stations where points are awarded based upon the total number of actions completed by the five team members. The team that earns the most points is the winner. If a team is shorthanded, count one of the middle scores from the team twice so the groups can be compared fairly.

Station	Points
1 Lay-ups from cone	15+ = 4 pt, 12-14 = 3 pt, 9-11 = 2 pt, 7-8 = 1 pt
2 Jump rope	900+ = 4 pt, 800-899 = 3 pt, 700-799 = 2 pt, 600-699 = 1 pt
3 Eraser shuttle	12+ = 4 pt, 11 = 3 pt, 10 = 2 pt, 9 = 1 pt
4 Sit-ups	140+ = 4 pt, 120-139 = 3 pt, 105-119 = 2 pt, 90-104 = 1 pt

5 VB wall pass	31+ = 4 pt, 27-30 = 3 pt, 23-26 = 2 pt, 19-22 = 1 pt
6 Push-ups	100+ = 4 pt, 80-99 = 3 pt, 70-79 = 2 pt, 60-69 = 1 pt
7 Skipping relay	9+ = 4 pt, 8 = 3 pt, 7 = 2 pt, 6 = 1 pt
8 Medicine ball pass	26+ = 4pt, 23-25 = 3 pt, 20-22 = 2 pt, 17-19 = 1 pt
9 Soccer wall pass	23+ = 4 pt, 18-22 = 3 pt, 15-17 = 2 pt, 12-14 = 1 pt
10 Basketball dribble	9+ = 4 pt, 8 = 3 pt, 7 = 2 pt, 6 = 1 pt

At station 3, the first person retrieves an eraser from a line 30 ft away and hands it to the second person, who brings it back to the original line and tags the next person. Each person rejoins the end of the line to go again if time permits. The score is the total number of people who complete a leg of the relay.

Because there are an odd number of people per team in this example, you or an assistant will hold legs at the sit-up station. You'll also announce when 40 sec have elapsed so that the other leg holders can change with the players who had been doing the sit-ups.

For the volleyball wall pass at station 5, participants form a line behind a cone. The first person passes overhead to the wall and runs to the end of the line. The second person passes the ball to the wall using a bump or overhead pass. The passer can move in front of the cone without penalty, if required. The number of successful passes determines the score. Should the ball hit the floor, the next person starts passing again from behind the cone, but the count resumes from the number of the last successful pass. To make this an actual drill, place a tape mark at a height of 9 ft and count only passes above that level.

All team members do push-ups at the same time; girls perform them with knees touching the mat. In the medicine ball pass, the team stands in a circle (marked by cones), and players pass the ball using a chest pass.

The soccer wall pass is similar to the volleyball wall pass, but players kick the ball from behind the cone. If the previous kick was not forceful enough so the ball rebounds far enough from the wall, the next person should dribble the ball behind the cone and then complete the pass. Players may not use their hands. If a player loses control, any team member may go after the ball and either dribble, kick, or pass it to the next person in the relay.

At station 10, players start at a designated line and dribble between each of the five cones spaced 5 ft apart. The total number of people to complete their turns determine the number of points the team earns.

Safety Considerations: Remind participants to pace themselves at the push-up and sit-up stations and to flex their elbows when catching the medicine ball. Be sure the eraser does not contain any chalk or the floor will become slippery.

Variations: While the actions in the game just described emphasize more serious sports skills, you can also choose unusual movements. You might have four players project a volleyball from a towel and try to make a basket while a fifth person retrieves them. Place balloons between team members in a line, and have them complete as many circuits around a cone as possible with their hands on their hips. Should a balloon drop, the group must stop and reposition the balloon before continuing. Give each team member a book to balance on her or his head and count how many successful trips to a designated line and back they can complete. Should the book fall off, the participant returns to the starting line.

Helpful Hints: At stations 2, 4, and 6, players will need extra time to tally the team's total number of executions. For stations 1, 5, 8, and 9 participants can keep track more easily if they call out the number of successful attempts as they occur. To add to the excitement, you can inform the class when 45 sec and 75 sec have elapsed. You can also record Beat the Clock scores and teams can see if they can improve their performances at a later time. The highest point total can serve as a benchmark for future teams.

Equipment Hints

Spasketball (p. 17): A makeshift goal can be constructed by placing a 1 in. × 7 ft piece of wood in each of two pylons and tying a rope between the tops of the wood strips.

Square Gymnastics (p. 23): Sources for the instrumental square dance records include Columbia Records for Educational Dance (XTV 62220) Bridgeport, CT; Square Dance Series Promenade and Do-Si-Do, "Turkey in the Straw," Dance Record Distributors (Folkcraft Records), 12 Fenwick St., Newark, NJ 07114; Educational Record Sales, 157 Chambers St., New York, NY 10007; Kimbro Records, P.O. Box 477, Long Beach, NJ 07740; and Educational Activities Inc., P.O. Box 382, Freeport, NY 11528.

Cupball (p. 43): An excellent source for cups that meet the desired specifications are stadiums or arenas in which sporting events take place. Another possibility is the housewares section in a department or variety store.

Towel Newcomb (p. 46): Players might find it easier for catching and throwing if a 1-in. hem is sewn down the short sides of each towel and a 1/2- to 3/4-in dowel approximately 26 in. long is inserted. This will keep the towel from tending to droop or sag if players are unable to apply the proper tension on the terrycloth.

Toppleball (p. 69): The easiest way to construct the post is to use a movable volleyball standard. If this is unavailable, embed a 6- to 8-ft, 4-in. diameter hollow metal pole in an old tire filled with concrete. For this homemade construction, you'll need to drill a hole in the post at the 4 ft level, just above the base, and thread a rope through this opening. Tie a knot at this end of the rope to prevent it from slipping back into the center of the post when the ball is toppled.

References and Suggested Sources

Appendix
B

Adams, J.L. (1986). *The care and feeding of ideas: A guide to encouraging creativity.* Reading, MA: Addison-Wesley Publishing Co.

Bok, D. (1986). *Higher learning.* Cambridge, MA: Harvard University Press.

Bratt, S. (1982). A process for teaching inventive games. *Florida Journal of Health, Physical Education and Recreation, 2,* 3-20.

Dietz, W.H., & Gortmaker, S.L. (1985). Do we fatten our children at the television set? Obesity and television viewing in children and adolescents. *Pediatrics, 75,* 807-812.

Fluegelman, A. (Ed.) (1976). *The new games book.* Garden City, NY: Dolphin Books/Doubleday & Co., Inc.

Haefele, J.W. (1962). *Creativity and innovation.* New York: Reinhold Publishing Corporation.

Holt, J. (1974). *Escape from childhood.* New York: Holt Associates.

Mooney, R., & Razik, T. (1967). *Explorations in creativity.* New York: Harper & Row Publishers, Inc.

Nieman, D.C. (1990). *Fitness and sports medicine: An introduction.* Palo Alto, CA: Bull Publishing Co.

Ochse, R. (1990). *Before the gates of excellence.* Cambridge, MA: Cambridge University Press.

Orlick, T. (1978). *The cooperative sports & games book.* New York: Pantheon Books.

Parnes, S.J., & Harding, H.F. (1962). *A source book for creative thinking.* New York: Scribner and Sons.

Porte, J. (1983). *Emerson essays and lectures.* New York: Literary Classics of America.

Reber, A.S. (1985). *The Penguin dictionary of psychology.* Harmondsworth, Middlesex: Penguin.

Sarason, S.B. (1990). *The predictable failure of educational reform.* San Francisco: Jossey-Bass.

Schlechty, P.C. (1990). *Schools for the 21st century.* San Francisco: Jossey-Bass.

Shank, R. (1988). *The creative attitude: Learning to ask and answer the right questions.* New York: Macmillan.

Silberman, C.E. (1970). *Crisis in the classroom: The remaking of American education.* New York: Random House.

Smith, C.F. (1935). *Games and game leadership.* New York: Dodd, Mead & Co.

Steinberg, R.J. (Ed.) (1988). *The nature of creativity.* Cambridge, MA: Cambridge University Press.

Toch, T. (1991). *In the name of excellence.* New York: Oxford University Press.

Tye, K.A., & Novotney, J.M. (1975). *Schools in transition: The practitioner as change agent.* New York: McGraw-Hill.

White, J.R. (Ed.) (1990). *Sports rules encyclopedia.* Champaign, IL: Human Kinetics.

Index

About the Author

Brenda Lichtman is a professor of kinesiology at Sam Houston State University in Huntsville, Texas. Since she began teaching in 1972, Brenda has worked to remedy the problem of stagnant and noncreative physical education curricula through the use of innovative games. She has delivered more than 45 presentations on innovative games at local, national, and international forums and has written scholarly articles on the subject as well. In addition, Brenda has put her ideas into practice by instituting a required innovative games class for kinesiology majors and minors at her university.

Brenda received her PhD in physical education from the University of Maryland at College Park in 1976. She has served as editor in chief of the *Journal of Educational Studies* and now sits on the editorial board of the *Texas Journal of Physical Education, Health, Recreation and Dance*. During her career, Brenda has twice been a finalist for the excellence in teaching award given by Sam Houston State University. She is a member of the Texas Alliance of Health, Physical Education, Recreation and Dance and the American Alliance of Health, Physical Education, Recreation and Dance. In her free time, Brenda enjoys cycling, backpacking, and playing pickleball.